MARY BERRY'S
COOKERY COURSE

MARY BERRY'S
COOKERY COURSE

DK

LONDON NEW YORK MUNICH
MELBOURNE DELHI

DK UK
Editor Polly Boyd
Project Art Editor Katherine Raj
Managing Editor Dawn Henderson
Managing Art Editor Christine Keilty
Design Concept Nicola Powling
Senior Jacket Creative Nicola Powling
Jacket Design Assistant Rosie Levine
Designer Harriet Yeomans
Design Assistant Kate Fenton
Pre-Production Producer Raymond Williams
Senior Producer Oliver Jeffreys
Creative Technical Support Sonia Charbonnier
Art Director Peter Luff
Recipe photography Tony Briscoe
Author photography Noel Murphy

DK INDIA
Editor Ligi John
Senior Art Editor Balwant Singh
Art Editors Anjan Dey, Vandna Sonkariya
Deputy Managing Editor Chitra Subramanyam
Managing Art Editor Navidita Thapa
Pre-Production Manager Sunil Sharma
DTP Designers Syed Md Farhan, Manish Upreti
Production Manager Pankaj Sharma

NOTE: The author and publisher advocate sustainable food choices, and every effort has been made to include only sustainable foods in this book. Food sustainability is, however, a shifting landscape, and so we encourage readers to keep up to date with advice on this subject, so that they are equipped to make their own ethical choices.

First published in Great Britain in 2013 by
Dorling Kindersley Limited
80 Strand, London WC2R 0RL

Penguin Group (UK)
2 4 6 8 10 9 7 5 3 1
001–188775–Jun/2013

A CIP catalogue record for this book is available
from the British Library.

ISBN 978-1-4093-6795-6

Colour reproduction by Alta Images
Printed and bound in Slovakia by TBB

Discover more at **www.dk.com**

Contents

Introduction

This book is for all home cooks who want to perfect their kitchen skills and get the very best from their cooking. Whether you're a completely new or more experienced cook, there is something for everyone. When selecting the recipes, I've gone back to basics – the classic recipes we all love, cooked simply. Some have an up-to-date twist or a shortcut, as I know the modern cook has to balance the desire to make delicious meals with a busy life outside the kitchen.

Each chapter starts with a "Master Recipe", featuring clear step-by-step photos and detailed descriptions of how to make each stage of the dish. These recipes are my favourites, and show you everything you need to achieve great results every time. In addition, I've selected over 100 other recipes for many occasions, with mini step-by-step photographs to show you the key techniques. In "Secrets of Success" I share my top tips to make cooking that much easier for you, while in the "Masterclass" features I demonstrate core skills such as roasting and carving meat, making pastry, and baking. I hope you find them useful.

My advice to every home cook, no matter how experienced, is to read through a recipe carefully a couple of times before you begin, to check you have all the correct ingredients and equipment and identify what you need to shop for. Every cook should keep a well-stocked cupboard of the basics – flour, sugar, baking powder, rice, pasta, chopped tomatoes – things that you will use often and that will keep. And have some back-up in the freezer of bread, milk, and stock. Always buy the finest ingredients you can afford and as locally produced as possible. I much prefer fresh herbs to dried, and remember you can grow many of them easily on your kitchen windowsill. Make sure you weigh accurately, as weighing is so important, especially when baking; use either imperial or metric measurements – do not mix the two for one recipe. All ovens vary, so be vigilant when it comes to temperatures and timings, and make a note of the exact timings for future use. Finally, perhaps the single most useful piece of advice I can give is when choosing a meal to serve to family or friends don't make it too complicated, especially if you're new to cooking. Keep it simple, follow the recipe, and you will be a star cook in no time!

Enjoy and best wishes,

Mary Berry

Basic Equipment

Good kitchen equipment will make preparation of ingredients and cooking easier, more pleasurable, and will also save you time. However, if you're a new cook don't feel you have to rush out and buy everything all at once. As your experience grows, you can gradually add to your collection. Always buy the best equipment you can afford; it is false economy to skimp at the outset, as cheap kitchenware won't last.

Pots and pans

Always choose pans that are heavy enough to sit securely on the hob without tipping, and bear in mind the type of hob you use. For instance, pans for induction hobs must be made from magnetizable metal, such as cast iron or steel, those for halogen hobs need to have thick bases that can cope with bursts of heat, and Aga pans benefit from very flat bases that make contact with the hot plates. I'd recommend having at least three deep saucepans of differing sizes and one shallow pan, ideally a sauté pan.

Medium pan Useful for a multitude of tasks, you'll need 3 of these of varying sizes, ideally 1.5 litres (2¾ pints), 2 litres (3½ pints), and 3 litres (5¼ pints) in capacity.

Large pan A 5-litre (8¾-pint) pan with a lid is useful for making soups and stocks and cooking pasta. It can also double up as a casserole.

Sauté pan More versatile and deeper than a frying pan, with straight sides and a lid, a sauté pan is useful for shallow-frying, boiling, and stir-frying.

Small (milk) pan With a capacity of about 1 litre (1¾ pints), a milk pan should be non-stick and have pouring lips on both sides.

Chargrill pan Cooking on a ridged pan (usually cast iron) on the hob is an easy way to achieve a professional-looking chargrilled result at home.

Wok Deep and made of very thin metal, this is the perfect pan for stir-frying, as the food cooks very quickly. Buy the largest you can, ideally with a single long handle and lid.

Omelette pan Useful if you make a lot of omelettes, as it is shallow and the right size (18–20cm/7–8in for a 2- or 3-egg omelette); if you don't have one, an ordinary frying pan will do.

Choice of materials for pots and pans

Pots and pans are available in a range of materials. The type you choose will have a significant effect on how food cooks, the pan's durability, and the cost. Over the years, manufacturers have developed cookware to improve its performance. Some pans are dishwasher safe (check the manufacturer's label for care instructions), but pans with wooden handles must be washed by hand.

MATERIAL	ADVANTAGES	DISADVANTAGES	IMPROVEMENTS
STAINLESS STEEL	Lightweight; durable; easy to clean; dishwasher safe; the best all-round choice for pots and pans	Poor heat distribution, unless combined with another metal; some food, such as eggs, can stick	The base of stainless-steel pans is usually sandwiched with another metal to improve heat distribution; pans with a heavy-gauge base are costly but will last a lifetime
CAST IRON	Durable; can be heated to very high temperatures, so good for cooking food quickly and evenly; also retains heat well, so ideal for slow-cooking too	Heavy to lift; takes a long time to heat up; requires effort to maintain (can rust and food can stick if the pan is not "seasoned" regularly); dishwasher can dull enamel	Cast-iron casseroles are often enamelled to prevent them from rusting
COPPER	Excellent heat conductor, so food cooks evenly, making copper the favourite of many chefs; attractive if well cared for	Expensive; heavy; copper reacts chemically with food, air, and liquid, so can discolour; needs polishing; not dishwasher safe	Copper pans are always lined with a non-reactive metal, most commonly stainless steel (formerly tin and silver)
ALUMINIUM	Good heat distribution; lightweight; affordable	Reacts to acidic foods; soft and scratches easily; not usually dishwasher safe (although some more expensive, treated pans may be – check the label)	Aluminium is usually covered with a non-reactive material, such as stainless steel or a non-stick coating. It is also often treated (anodized) to harden
NON-STICK COATING	Food does not stick, so less fat can be used, making it a healthy option; the non-stick surface is also easy to clean	Easily scratched; coating can wear off with time; cannot use metal cooking implements or an abrasive sponge or scrubbing brush; not always dishwasher safe	Some newer versions, such as titanium, are more durable than a traditional non-stick coating, and can be used with metal utensils without scratching

Basic Equipment

Ovenware

Metal is the best conductor of heat, and is therefore ideal for baking (including pastry). Dishes made of earthenware, stoneware, porcelain, and heatproof glass can also be used in the oven, and are often attractive enough to bring to the table.

Muffin or Yorkshire pudding tin Has 6 or 12 holes; the width and depth of the holes are variable.

Springform cake tin Enables delicate cakes, such as cheesecakes, to be removed easily.

Ramekin A small ceramic baking dish, ideal for individual soufflés and crème caramels; average capacity is 150ml (5fl oz).

Pie tin This has plain, sloping sides and a lip for the pie edging. A good all-purpose size is 23cm (9in) across the top.

Wire rack Essential for cooling cakes and biscuits, as it allows air to circulate around them.

Baking sheet A flat metal tray used for baking biscuits and other small items. Buy the heavy-duty type, and the largest that will fit in your oven.

Sandwich/sponge tin Shallow cake tin; the most useful size is 20cm (8in) and at least 3cm (1¼in) deep. Many (but not all) have a removable base.

Quiche tin Choose one with a removable base, so the quiche can be removed from the tin without breaking.

Loaf tin Useful for making pâtés and terrines as well as baking bread and cakes. The most useful capacity is 450g (1lb) or 900g (2lb).

Traybake tin For baking cakes and biscuits that are cut into squares for serving; 30 x 23cm (12 x 9in) and 4cm (1½in) deep.

Baking dish Usually made of stoneware or ceramic. Most baking dishes can be put under the grill as well as into a hot oven, but cannot go on the hob.

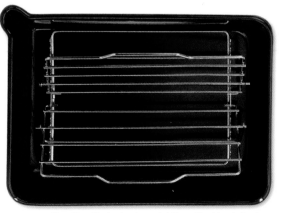

Casserole An enamelled cast-iron casserole retains heat well and is flameproof, so it can be used on the hob as well as in the oven.

Roasting tin A sturdy metal tin with sides is best for roasting meat and vegetables. Some are equipped with a rack, enabling meat to be roasted free of its fat. Can be used on the hob.

Cutting tools

A set of good-quality, sharp knives is vital. Store knives in a block or on a wall-mounted magnetic strip; if kept in a drawer, they go blunt quickly. Ceramic knives – the latest in knife technology – are lighter, harder, and sharper than steel blades, but they're not suitable for everything, including carving, boning, and jointing poultry and meat.

Scissors Keep a pair solely for kitchen use. Handy for many tasks, such as snipping herbs.

Serrated knife Ideal for slicing tomatoes or lemons, and other vegetables and fruit with slippery or tough skins.

Bread knife A serrated knife with a 21cm (8¼in) blade that penetrates crusts cleanly.

Poultry shears These make light work of jointing chicken and other birds.

Paring knife For fine work, such as peeling and cutting cores from apples and peppers. The blade is 10cm (4in) long.

Carving fork and knife The fork keeps the meat steady, while the knife is useful for carving meat into thin slices.

Chef's knife The all-purpose chopping knife, with a rigid, heavy, 20cm (8in) blade.

Knife sharpener Sharpen knives every few days; blunt knives can cause accidents.

Mezzaluna Works by being rocked over the food to be chopped; particularly useful for large quantities of tender-leaved herbs.

Chopping board Use a solid wooden chopping board in combination with one of a set of flexible cutting mats placed on top; each mat is colour-coded to avoid cross-contamination.

Peeler A swivel blade (left) is best for straight-sided vegetables; a fixed blade for round ones.

Measuring equipment

Buying and using good measuring equipment will always pay off, especially when it comes to baking pies, bread, or cakes, when accuracy is so important for successful results.

Automatic timer Useful when you're busy and forget to watch the clock.

Measuring jug For measuring liquids and some dry ingredients. Toughened glass is better than plastic for hot liquids.

Measuring spoons Invest in a set of measuring spoons; ordinary ones are not accurate enough.

Meat thermometer Insert the probe through the thickest part of the meat at the start of cooking.

Scales Buy a really good set of digital scales if you're planning to do a lot of baking. Mechanical scales are cheaper but less precise.

Basic Equipment

Bowls and utensils

There is a vast, often bewildering, range of kitchen equipment available, including the latest "must-have" gadgets. Some are useful, others less so. Here is some equipment that I use regularly.

Mixing bowls A range of different-sized bowls is essential for a variety of kitchen tasks.

Tongs Useful for turning and moving delicate pieces of hot food without piercing it as a fork would do; helpful when chargrilling.

Cutters For stamping out scones, biscuits, and tartlet cases; edges may be plain or fluted.

Slotted spoon For removing food from liquids and for skimming fat or scum off the surface of stocks or soups. Also essential for draining fat or oil from food you have fried.

Colander Choose a freestanding, sturdy colander with handles for safe draining of vegetables and pasta.

Flexible spatula Scrapes bowls clean, and is good for folding mixtures.

Fish slice Very useful for turning or serving delicate foods that tend to break up easily, such as fish and eggs.

Wire whisk Incorporates air into a mixture; used for whisking egg whites and whipping cream; hand-held electric whisks are also available.

Serving spoon Metal spoons are good for serving but not for cooking, as they will scratch pans; some spoons have holes for draining excess liquid.

Wooden spoons For many tasks, including mixing; long-handled spoons are best for stirring on the hob. Corner spoons reach the very edges of the pan.

Ladle To avoid pouring hot liquids from heavy pans, use a ladle for serving soups and stews.

Palette knife Useful for spreading (for instance icing a cake) and for turning and lifting foods.

Sieves The best material for a sieve is stainless steel, as it is strong, dishwasher safe, and will not rust. Ideally, have two sieves: one large and one small.

Wooden rolling pin Choose a long, heavy type, ideally 5–7cm (2–3in) in diameter and without handles, as they can make indents in the pastry.

Skewers Short metal skewers are useful for testing for doneness and trussing; long wooden skewers are best for kebabs.

Pastry brush For glazing and sealing pastry, greasing cake tins, and brushing foods with oil. Ideally have two, for different tasks.

Piping bag and nozzle For piping cream and icings, and for shaping meringues and éclairs. Metal nozzles are more accurate than plastic ones and create a sharper edge.

Processing tools

Having the right processing tools means wasting less food. Electric processors can often save you time, but they can be costly to buy, and take up valuable storage space. Think carefully about what you cook, how often, and the quantities involved before investing in them.

Box grater The most useful all-purpose grater, with different-sized holes on each face, ranging from large (for grating cheese) to very fine (for hard items, such as Parmesan or nutmeg).

Pestle and mortar Typically made of stone or ceramic; for grinding herbs, spices, and garlic, and for making sauces such as pesto.

Lemon squeezer Choose one with a well-fitted strainer to catch the pips, and a sturdy bowl to hold the liquid.

Garlic press A detachable grille makes cleaning the press much easier.

Potato masher Must be strong with a comfortable handle. For really light, fluffy results, use a ricer.

Hand-held blender Will purée soup directly in a pan. Less expensive, more compact, and easier to wash up than a freestanding blender.

Freestanding blender Also known as a liquidizer, this makes smooth soups, sauces, and fruit and vegetable purées. Quicker and better for large quantities than a hand-held blender.

Food processor Different blades chop, grate, slice, and purée all kinds of ingredients; can also be used to make pastry and bread dough.

Technique Finder

Use this visual guide to help you find key cooking techniques at a glance. Many are basic skills for all home cooks, while others are more specific and challenging.

Stocks

Chicken stock, making fresh, p126

Beef stock, making fresh, p146

Fish stock, making fresh, p58

Vegetable stock, making fresh, p30

Hot stock, using, p198

Eggs

Testing eggs for freshness, p74

Separating eggs, p54

Whisking egg whites, p276

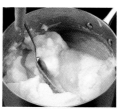

Folding egg whites into a mixture, p50

Soft-boiling eggs, p74

Hard-boiling and shelling eggs, p86

Poaching eggs, p80

Scrambling eggs, p76

Making omelettes, pp70–72

Making soufflés, pp48–50

Dairy

Hot milk, using, p94

Cheese, grating, p196

Cream, whipping, p284

Whipped cream, filling a piping bag, p301

Whipped cream, piping, p301

Fish and shellfish

Flatfish (sole), filleting and skinning, p106

Monkfish, filleting and trimming, p100

Tuna steaks, chargrilling, p246

Salmon, chargrilling, p92

Salmon (oven-poached), skinning and preparing for serving, p104

Fishcakes, forming and pan-frying, p108

Clams, cleaning, p44

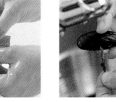

Mussels, preparing, p200

Prawns, peeling and deveining, p64

Scallops, trimming and slicing, p62

Poultry and meat

Chicken breasts, preparing, p130

Chicken livers, trimming, p56

Chicken (cooked), stripping meat off the bones, p28

Poultry, stuffing, p129

Chicken, roasting, pp112–14

Roast chicken, carving, p128

Roast duck or goose, carving, p129

Roasting tin, oiling, p118

Casserole (game), thickening the sauce, p136

Beef burgers, shaping, p148

Meatballs, shaping and frying, p154

Beef mince, browning, p166

Beef Wellington, making, p150

Beef (sirloin), roasting, pp152–53

Beef (sirloin), carving, p152

Technique Finder

Poultry and meat (continued)

Beef (silverside), pot-roasting, p152

Bacon, slicing and frying, p88

Pork (fillet/tenderloin), slicing for stir-fry, p160

Pork (boned joint), stuffing, p165

Pork (shoulder), roasting, pp164–65

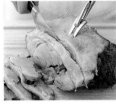

Pork (shoulder), carving, p164

Lamb (rack), trimming, p176

Lamb (boned joint), stuffing, p171

Lamb (leg), roasting, pp170–71

Lamb (leg), carving, p170

Vegetables

Potatoes, peeling, p208

Potatoes, slicing thinly, p208

Potatoes, dicing, p220

New potatoes, scrubbing, p238

Potatoes, boiling for mashing, p162

Potatoes, mashing, p166

Potatoes, roasting, p172

Carrots, cutting into sticks, p160

Carrots, cutting into rounds, p168

Onion, chopping, p188

Onion, slicing, p162

Onion, frying, p94

Shallots, peeling, p124

Shallots, chopping, p132

Spring onions, slicing for stir-fries, p218

Garlic, peeling and chopping, p52

Garlic, crushing, p208

Leeks, preparing, p230

Asparagus, trimming, p54

Celery, trimming, p42

French beans, topping, tailing, and slicing, p42

Peas, shelling, p212

Tomatoes (cherry), preparing, p196

Tomatoes, skinning and deseeding, p216

Avocado, preparing, p240

Sweetcorn, dehusking, p44

Courgettes, deseeding, p212

Butternut squash, deseeding, p34

Red pepper, coring and deseeding, p216

Red pepper, cutting into wedges, p118

Mediterranean vegetables, roasting, pp204–206

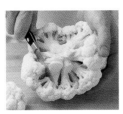

Cauliflower, cutting into florets, p230

Cabbage (red), coring and shredding, p210

Cabbage (savoy), preparing, p42

Watercress, washing and chopping, p36

Cucumber, deseeding, p98

Mushrooms, cleaning, trimming, and slicing, p194

Porcini, soaking, p198

Tofu, preparing for stir-frying, p226

Beansprouts, picking over and rinsing, p160

Technique Finder

Pasta, rice, couscous, and pulses

Penne (dried), cooking, p186

Chinese egg noodles (dried), softening, p116

Rice (white long-grain), cooking, p120

Couscous, cooking, p178

Kidney beans (dried), soaking and cooking, p242

Red lentils, preparing and cooking, p224

"The way you prepare food really makes a difference. It affects the way it cooks, its texture, and even its taste."

Herbs, spices, and seeds

Basil, shredding, p216

Chives, snipping, p82

Coriander, chopping, p28

Parsley, chopping, p82

Dill, chopping, p98

Mint, chopping, p176

Rosemary, chopping, p168

Tarragon, chopping, p238

Bouquet garni, making, p136

Chillies, deseeding and chopping, p156

Ginger, peeling and chopping, p220

Nutmeg, grating using a microplane grater, p56

Nutmeg, grating using a nutmeg grater, p26

Pine nuts, toasting, p250

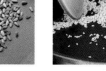
Sesame seeds, toasting, p218

Fruit

Apples, coring, p210

Apples, slicing, p210

Lemon, squeezing, p296

Lemon zest, grating, p262

Mango, destoning and slicing, p280

Mango, dicing, p280

Oranges, segmenting, p270

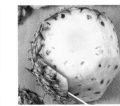
Pineapple, peeling and coring, p270

Pineapple, slicing, p270

Strawberries, hulling and washing, p268

Puddings and pies

Shortcrust pastry, making, p272

Pâte sucrée, making, p273

Quick puff pastry, making, p273

Pastry, rolling out, p254

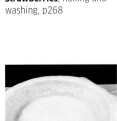
Pie tin, lining, p255

Pie edge, crimping, p256

Pastry case, blind baking, p274

Batter (for pancakes/ Yorkshire puddings), making, p228

Pancakes, cooking, p260

Meringues, making, p278

Crumble, making the topping, p258

Sticky Toffee Pudding, making the mixture, p264

Crème caramel, filling the ramekins, p288

Chocolate, melting, p286

Chocolate, making curls, p286

Technique Finder

Cakes and biscuits

Cake tins, greasing and lining, p300

Cake, making the mixture and baking, p300

Cake, testing for doneness, p300

Biscuits, crushing, p284

Carrot cake, making the mixture, p302

Shortbread, making the dough, p320

Flapjacks, making the mixture, p314

Choux pastry, making, p322

Scones, making the dough, p312

Chocolate-chip cookies, spooning out the dough, p318

Fruit cake, testing for doneness, p304

Blueberry muffins, baking, p310

Chocolate frosting, making, p308

Icing for cupcakes, making, p298

Cake, applying the icing, p301

Bread, breadcrumbs, and croûtons

Bread dough, making, pp326–27

Focaccia dough, covering, p334

Pizza base, making, p340

Breadcrumbs (fresh), making, p96

Croûtons, making, p234

Sauces and dressings

Custard, making, p266

French dressing (vinaigrette), making, p236

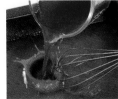

Gravy, making, p114 and p138

Hollandaise sauce, making, p80

Marie Rose sauce, making, p66

Sauces and dressings (continued)

Mayonnaise (traditional), making, p248

Mayonnaise (quick), making, p248

Pesto (traditional), making, p38

Pesto (quick), making, p38

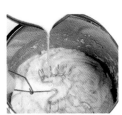

White sauce, making, p190

Tomato sauce, making, p188

Onion marmalade, making, pp142-43

"If you master the classic sauces, there's no end to the number of recipes you can make with them."

GLOSSARY OF COOKING METHODS AND TECHNIQUES

I have kept specialist cooking terms to a minimum in the recipes, but it is useful to familiarize yourself with basic culinary terms. Those that occur in this book are defined below, and many are also illustrated on the recipe pages.

Bake To cook in the oven.

Baste To moisten roasting meat or fish by spooning over hot fat and juices.

Beat To work a mixture smooth with a regular, hard, rhythmic movement.

Blanch To dip food quickly into boiling water.

Blind bake To bake a pie or tart with a false filling of baking parchment or beans before it is filled to create a crisper crust.

Bring to the boil To heat liquid on the hob until it bubbles vigorously.

Brown To partially cook meat by frying it quickly until the surface is brown; this improves colour and seals the meat's juices.

Chargrill To cook food on a hot cast-iron chargrill pan set on the hob.

Coat To roll or dip food in a coating, such as flour, eggs, or breadcrumbs.

Crimp To pinch the edges of a pie for a fluted effect.

Dice To cut food into tiny, regular pieces.

Drizzle To slowly pour a liquid, such as icing, oil, or vinegar, in a fine stream, back and forth over food.

Dust To sprinkle food with a dry ingredient, such as flour or sugar.

Fillet To take a fish off the bone, resulting in fillets.

Fold/fold in To combine a light ingredient, such as egg whites, with a heavier mixture by cutting through vertically and turning one part over the other.

Fry/pan-fry To cook food in a little oil or butter on top of the hob.

Grease To spread a little fat over the inside of a tin or dish to prevent sticking.

Grill To cook by exposure under a direct heat.

Knead To press dough with the heel of your hand so the dough becomes elastic.

Marinate To soak foods in a flavoured liquid mixture, either sweet or savoury.

Parboil To boil until partially cooked.

Pipe To force icing or whipped cream through a bag and nozzle to create decorative swirls.

Poach To cook delicate foods, such as eggs or fish, in hot liquid, gently and below boiling point.

Pot-roast/braise To brown meat in fat first, then cook it slowly in a covered pan with a little liquid.

Preheat To heat the oven or grill to the stated temperature before using.

Purée To blend food in a blender or food processor, or force it through a sieve, for a smooth texture.

Reduce To evaporate some of the liquid in a sauce by boiling it quickly.

Roast To cook food using hot, dry air, usually in an oven and with added fat.

Roux A blend of flour and fat, heated, blended, and used to thicken sauces.

Sauté To fry food quickly in a small amount of fat.

Shred To cut food, such as lettuce, cabbage, or basil, into slender strips.

Simmer To cook food gently, just below boiling point; bubbles almost or only just break the surface.

Skim To remove fat or froth from the surface of liquid, such as stock.

Stir-fry To fry food very quickly in a hot wok or a sauté pan using little oil.

Strain To pass liquid through a sieve.

Sweat To sauté over a low heat with a lid on.

Toast To brown food, such as seeds, either in the oven or in a dry pan on the hob.

Trim To cut off unwanted parts of vegetables or meat before cooking.

Truss To tie poultry legs with string or skewers to ensure they stay together during cooking and to keep stuffing in place.

Whip/whisk To beat ingredients, such as cream or eggs, until light and fluffy using a wire whisk.

Soups

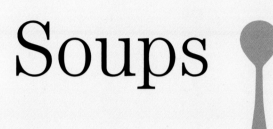

Leek and Potato Soup

A good home-made soup tastes so much better than a bought one, and this is quick and easy to make. It freezes well too. Serve with chunks of crusty bread for a homely lunch or supper, or swirl in a little extra cream for an elegant first course. When leek and potato soup is served chilled, it is known as vichyssoise.

 Serves 4   **Prep** 25 mins   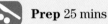 **Cook** 30 mins

Ingredients

3 leeks (about 250g/9oz)
1 onion
25g (scant 1oz) butter
500g (1lb 2oz) potatoes
1.2 litres (2 pints) hot chicken stock
   (see p126)
salt and freshly ground
   black pepper
nutmeg
150ml (5fl oz) single cream
1 tsp lemon juice
2 tbsp chopped fresh parsley
   or snipped chives, to garnish

Special equipment
A 5-litre (8¾-pint) pan and
an electric blender

PER SERVING
Calories: 293
Saturated fat: 8g
Unsaturated fat: 4g
Sodium: 349mg

Cook's notes

Make the stock

I have recommended using a good home-made chicken stock here to give depth of flavour, but vegetable stock (see p30) can be used instead. It will give a lighter taste.

Prepare ahead

You can make the soup and keep it in the fridge, covered, for up to 3 days, or frozen for up to 3 months. If making vichyssoise, leave to cool, then cover and chill for at least 4 hours. Chilling dulls the flavour, so check the seasoning before serving.

Prepare the leeks and onion

 Prep 10 mins

Trim the leeks, leaving some green at the top to colour the soup. Cut in half lengthways, then cut across into 5mm (¼in) slices. Rinse in a colander in plenty of cold running water. Drain well. Peel the onion and cut it into slices about the same thickness as the leeks.

Sweat the vegetables

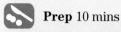 **Prep** 10 mins   **Cook** 10 mins

KEY to SUCCESS Make sure you don't have the heat too high, or the butter may burn.

1 Place the pan on the hob over a medium heat and add the butter. Once the butter has melted and is foaming, add the chopped leeks and onion.

2 Stir to coat the vegetables in butter. Cover the pan and cook for about 10 minutes, or until soft but not brown, lifting the lid occasionally to stir.

3 While the leeks and onion are cooking, peel the potatoes and cut them into 5mm (¼in) slices. When the leeks and onion are ready, add the potato slices to the pan.

Add the liquid

Cook 15 mins

KEY to SUCCESS Make sure all the ingredients are totally soft before you purée them. Any undercooked vegetables will make a lumpy soup.

1 As soon as you have added the potatoes, pour in the hot stock, then add a little salt and pepper. Do not use too much salt because the stock may already contain some.

2 Add about 8 gratings of nutmeg, turn up the heat, and bring to the boil. Reduce the heat, cover, and simmer for about 10 minutes, or until the vegetables are soft.

Blend and reheat

Prep 5 mins   **Cook** 5 mins

KEY to SUCCESS If using a hand-held blender, keep the blades held below the level of the soup to prevent splashes, and blend for about 3 minutes.

1 Remove the pan from the heat and purée using an electric hand-held blender. Or, allow the soup to cool slightly and use a freestanding blender, puréeing in batches.

2 Bring the soup to a boil over a medium heat. Take the pan off the heat, add the cream and lemon juice, then stir and check the seasoning. Garnish with fresh herbs.

"A swirl of cream and light sprinkling of herbs make a soup look so fresh and appetizing."

Chicken Noodle Soup

Being both light and filling, this Asian-style soup is ideal for lunch. Browning the meat and vegetables gives good colour and depth of flavour to the stock. Once strained, the stock can be used as a base for other types of chicken soup too.

Ingredients

Serves 4

1½ tbsp vegetable or sunflower oil
6 chicken drumsticks, about
 675g (1½lb) in total
1 onion, peeled and roughly chopped
2 carrots, peeled (1 thickly sliced,
 1 diced)
1 celery stick, trimmed and sliced
2.5cm (1in) piece of fresh root ginger,
 peeled
2 garlic cloves, peeled and sliced
85g (3oz) dried medium Chinese egg
 or rice noodles
198g can sweetcorn, drained
salt and freshly ground black pepper
splash of soy sauce
4 spring onions, trimmed and shredded
fresh chopped coriander or flat-leaf
 parsley, to garnish

PER SERVING

Calories: 354
Saturated fat: 2.5g
Unsaturated fat: 9.5g
Sodium: 548mg

Method

1 Heat 1 tablespoon of the oil in a large pan. Put in the drumsticks and fry over a medium heat for 5–8 minutes until browned all over. Do this in 2 batches, if necessary. Remove the drumsticks and set aside.

2 Make the stock: add the remaining oil to the pan with the onion, sliced carrot, and celery and fry for 4–5 minutes until the onions are just starting to brown. Add the browned chicken. Pour in 1.5 litres (2¾ pints) water, bring to the boil, then simmer gently, covered, for 40–45 minutes.

3 Skim off any froth from the surface with a slotted spoon. Lift out the drumsticks and set aside. Strain the stock through a fine sieve.

4 When the drumsticks are cool, strip off the meat, as shown below, and set aside. Pour the stock into a large pan. Drop in the ginger, garlic, and diced carrot and simmer gently for 10 minutes.

5 Remove the ginger and garlic with a slotted spoon and discard. Drop the noodles into the stock and simmer for 4–5 minutes until tender. Stir in the sweetcorn and chicken, warm through, then season with salt and pepper and a splash of soy sauce.

6 Ladle into warmed bowls and scatter over the spring onions and chopped coriander or parsley.

Strip meat off the bones

Using your fingers and a knife, tear and cut the meat from the bones. Trim the tendons and discard the skin. Shred the meat with your fingers.

Chop the coriander

Strip the leaves from the stalks and make a pile of the leaves. Chop them by holding the knife tip still and rocking the handle up and down.

Curried Parsnip Soup

This is a variation on food writer Jane Grigson's original parsnip soup recipe, created when she had a glut of parsnips in her garden. Prepare the parsnips just before using, because they have a tendency to discolour once peeled and cut.

Ingredients

Serves 4

3 tbsp sunflower oil
1 onion, peeled and chopped
1 tsp Madras (hot) curry powder
10g (¼oz) plain flour
900ml (1½ pints) vegetable
    stock
500g (1lb 2oz) parsnips, peeled
    and sliced
salt and freshly ground black pepper
1-2 tsp lemon juice

FOR THE CORIANDER YOGURT

150g (5½oz) plain Greek yogurt
2 tbsp finely chopped fresh
    coriander leaves

PER SERVING

Calories: 226
Saturated fat: 3g
Unsaturated fat: 12g
Sodium: 1072mg

Method

1 Heat the oil in a large pan. Add the onion and cook over a medium heat for about 5 minutes, or until softened. Sprinkle the curry powder and flour over the onion, stir well, then pour in the stock and bring to the boil over a high heat, stirring all the time.

2 Add the parsnips and salt and pepper and bring back to the boil. Reduce the heat, cover, and simmer for 15 minutes, or until the parsnips are very tender.

3 Remove the pan from the heat. Using a blender, purée the soup for about 3 minutes until smooth. You may need to do this in batches.

4 Return the soup to a medium heat and bring to a simmer. Add a little lemon juice, to taste. Check the seasoning.

5 Make the coriander yogurt: put the yogurt and chopped coriander leaves into a small bowl and mix until thoroughly combined.

6 Stir the soup one more time, then ladle it into warmed bowls. Top each serving with a spoonful of coriander yogurt.

VARIATION Curried Carrot Soup Replace the parsnips in the main recipe with the same quantity of carrots.

How I make fresh vegetable stock

1 Chop 2 onions, 1 leek, 3 celery stalks, and 2–3 carrots. Put into a large pan and add 1 bouquet garni plus 1 crushed garlic clove, if you like.

2 Cover completely with water and bring to the boil. Skim off any scum that rises to the surface, then lower the heat and simmer for 30 minutes.

3 Strain the stock. If not using immediately, leave to cool, cover, and store in the fridge for up to 5 days or the freezer for up to 6 months.

Mary's Secrets of Success

Soups

1 **Soup tastes so much better** made from a good homemade stock. Whenever I roast a chicken I make stock afterwards and freeze it in 300ml or 600ml cream cartons.

Chicken Noodle Soup, pp28–29

2 **Stock cubes can be rather salty,** so if you use them I recommend that you go easy on the salt.

3 **If using a freestanding blender** for puréeing, allow the soup to cool slightly before putting it into the jug or it may crack.

4 **For an ultra-smooth texture,** pass puréed soup through a large sieve.

5 **If using flour as a thickener,** blend it with cold stock or water before whisking it in; if added to the hot liquid, it will go lumpy.

Watercress Soup, pp36–37

6 **An attractive garnish** always really lifts a soup. Try adding fresh herbs (chopped or whole leaves), sliced spring onions, toasted nuts or seeds, croûtons, crispy fried bacon, or finely grated citrus zest.

7 **Cream is delicious added to soups,** but single and soured cream and yogurt will curdle if added to hot liquid, so it's best to use double cream or full-fat crème fraîche.

Clam Chowder, pp44–45

8 **If freezing soup,** don't add cream, milk, or eggs until the reheating stage. Label the container clearly with the name and date. Frozen soups all look very similar!

9 **If you have frozen soup,** defrost it and gently heat in a pan over a low heat. If the soup is starting to separate, whisk it quickly or blend until smooth.

10 **If feeding a lot of people** I find it quicker and less messy to pour soup from a large jug with a good spout rather than using a ladle.

Easy Tomato Soup with Pesto, pp38–39

Spiced Butternut Squash Soup

Colourful and smooth, with a touch of spice, this is a great autumn and winter warmer. For a change of texture, I keep a few pieces of the roasted squash back, cut them into little cubes, then stir them into the puréed soup when reheating.

Ingredients

Serves 6

1 butternut squash, about 1.1kg (2½lb)
2 tsp ground coriander
1 tsp ground cumin
3 tbsp olive oil, plus 2 tsp extra
    for frying
¼ tsp dried crushed chillies
salt and freshly ground black pepper
25g (scant 1oz) butter
1 large onion, peeled and roughly
    chopped
2 carrots, about 350g (12oz) in total,
    peeled and roughly chopped
1 celery stick, trimmed and roughly
    chopped
2 garlic cloves, peeled and chopped
1.4 litres (2½ pints) vegetable stock
    (see p30) or chicken stock (see p126)
finely chopped flat-leaf parsley,
    to garnish

PER SERVING

Calories: 226
Saturated fat: 3g
Unsaturated fat: 7g
Sodium: 307mg

Method

1 Preheat the oven to 200°C (fan 180°C/400°F/Gas 6). Deseed the butternut squash as shown below, then peel using a small, sharp knife to remove the skin. Cut the squash into wedges and put into a roasting tin.

2 Put the coriander and cumin into a bowl with the oil and pour it over the squash. Scatter the chillies over the squash, toss together to coat, then spread in a single layer. Season with salt and pepper. Roast for 35–40 minutes, or until tender.

3 Meanwhile, melt the butter with the remaining 2 teaspoons of oil in a large pan. Add the onion, carrots, celery, and garlic and fry for 5–8 minutes, or until the onion is beginning to soften.

4 Pour in 1 litre (1¾ pints) stock, bring to the boil, then lower the heat and simmer, covered, for 20–25 minutes until the vegetables are soft.

5 Break up the roasted squash into smaller pieces to make it easier for puréeing, then scrape and stir the contents of the roasting tin into the pan with the other vegetables. Purée the soup until smooth.

6 Return the soup to the pan and pour in enough of the remaining stock to give the consistency you like. Taste for seasoning, then warm through and serve scattered with a little parsley.

How to deseed butternut squash

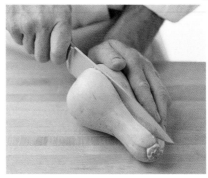

1 Place the squash on a work surface and, holding it firmly, use a chef's knife to cut it in half lengthways.

2 Using a spoon, scrape around the centre of each squash half to remove the seeds and fibres. Discard.

Watercress Soup

With its beautiful vivid green appearance and unusual peppery flavour, this soup makes an elegant first course for a dinner party. To preserve the soup's colour, don't keep it hot for too long on the hob and serve it as soon as possible.

Ingredients

Serves 4

50g (1¾oz) butter
1 large potato (about 300g/10oz),
   peeled and roughly chopped
1 large onion, peeled and chopped
450ml (15fl oz) chicken stock
   (see p126)
salt and freshly ground black pepper
200g (7oz) watercress, chopped
500ml (16fl oz) milk
1–2 tbsp lemon juice
4 tbsp single cream, to garnish

PER SERVING

Calories: 314
Saturated fat: 12g
Unsaturated fat: 6g
Sodium: 303mg

Method

1 Melt the butter in a large pan. Add the potato and onion and stir to mix. Cover and cook over a low heat for 15 minutes, stirring occasionally.

2 Pour in the stock and bring to the boil over a high heat. Add salt and pepper, cover, and reduce the heat. Simmer for about 10 minutes, or until the potatoes are very tender.

3 Remove the pan from the heat and add the watercress. Using a blender or food processor, purée the soup until smooth.

4 Return the soup to a medium heat, pour in the milk, and stir well to mix. Bring the soup to just simmering point.

5 Add a little lemon juice, taste the soup and add more lemon juice if you like. Check the seasoning and add more if necessary.

6 Stir the soup one more time, then either ladle or pour it into 4 warmed bowls. Spoon 1 tablespoon cream in the centre of each bowl of soup to decorate and swirl it in.

VARIATION Spinach Soup Use the same quantity of young spinach as watercress and remove any tough stalks before chopping. Omit the lemon juice and add a few gratings of nutmeg with the salt and pepper in step 2.

Prepare the watercress

Divide the watercress sprigs, wash and dry them, then strip the leaves from the stalks. Pile the leaves on a chopping board and chop them coarsely.

Easy Tomato Soup with Pesto

Tomatoes and pesto are the perfect flavour partnership for this soup, and the home-made pesto keeps in the fridge for about 2 weeks, so you can make it ahead. For an even easier soup when time is short, buy a good-quality fresh pesto.

Ingredients

Serves 4

1 vegetable stock cube
25g (scant 1oz) butter
1 onion, peeled and finely chopped
25g (scant 1oz) plain flour
2 x 400g cans chopped tomatoes
2 tbsp tomato purée
salt and freshly ground black pepper
1 tsp caster sugar
small basil leaves, to garnish

FOR THE PESTO

60g (2oz) basil leaves, shredded
1 garlic clove, peeled and crushed
60g (2oz) pine nuts
salt and freshly ground black pepper
60g (2oz) Parmesan cheese, grated
4 tbsp olive oil

PER SERVING

Calories: 128
Saturated fat: 3g
Unsaturated fat: 2g
Sodium: 648mg

USING PESTO

Pesto freezes really well, without any loss of flavour or colour, so you can make up large quantities of the sauce, freeze it in batches, and defrost just as much as you need each time. If using shop-bought pesto, simply add 6-8 tablespoons to the soup at the end.

Method

1 Dissolve the stock cube in 425ml (14½fl oz) boiling water. Melt the butter in a large pan, add the onion, and cook over a low heat for 10 minutes or until soft, stirring occasionally.

2 Sprinkle the flour over the onion, stir well, then add the stock, tomatoes, tomato purée, and salt and pepper. Bring to the boil over a high heat, stirring all the time, then simmer for 2–3 minutes, stirring occasionally. Leave to cool slightly.

3 Place a large sieve over a large heatproof bowl, pour the soup into the sieve, and press the solids through with the back of a spoon. Do not use a blender: sieving the soup will remove tomato cores and seeds.

4 Pour the soup back into the pan, return to medium heat, and bring to a simmer. Add the sugar, check the seasoning, and swirl a tablespoon or two of pesto into each bowl before serving. Garnish with basil leaves.

VARIATION **Red Pepper and Tomato Soup** Omit one of the cans of tomatoes and at step 2 add 400g (14oz) of chargrilled red peppers (see p186, step 1).

Traditional pesto

Pound the basil, garlic, pine nuts, and seasoning in a pestle and mortar. Tip into a bowl and add half the cheese and a little oil, mix, then add the remaining cheese and oil. Blend well.

Pesto the quick way

Purée all the dry ingredients in a food processor until almost smooth. With the blades turning, add the oil gradually, in a thin, steady stream until the sauce thickens and emulsifies.

We often have soup for lunch. I make it well ahead, sometimes in batches and freeze, so all I have to do for a quick lunch is thaw and reheat.

Minestrone

With all the fresh vegetables and pasta in this soup, it's a meal in itself. You can ring the changes by using different vegetables to suit different seasons, providing the total amount of vegetables you use is about the same as in this recipe.

Ingredients

Serves 4–6

2 tbsp olive oil
1 onion, peeled and finely chopped
1 carrot, peeled and chopped
1 celery stick, trimmed and
    finely chopped
1 leek, trimmed and thinly sliced
25g (scant 1oz) plain flour
1.5 litres (2¾ pints) chicken stock
    (see p126)
400g can chopped tomatoes
salt and freshly ground black pepper
50g (1¾oz) dried spaghetti, broken
    into short lengths
100g (3½oz) French beans, trimmed
    and cut into 2.5cm (1in) lengths
100g (3½oz) savoy cabbage, shredded
grated Parmesan cheese, to serve

PER SERVING

Calories: 243
Saturated fat: 2g
Unsaturated fat: 7g
Sodium: 373mg

SMALL PASTA FOR SOUPS

Small pasta, or "pastina", is available in a variety of attractive shapes for soups and includes conchigliette (small shells), stelline (tiny stars), ditali (small tubes), and orzo (small pasta that resembles grains of rice).

Method

1 Heat the oil in a large pan. Add the onion, carrot, celery, and leek and cook over a low heat for 5 minutes, stirring frequently, until the vegetables are softened.

2 Sprinkle in the flour and stir to mix. Add the stock, tomatoes, and salt and pepper and bring to the boil over a high heat, stirring constantly. Partially cover, reduce the heat, and simmer for 20 minutes.

3 Drop the spaghetti, beans, and cabbage into the pan, stir well, and cook for 10 minutes, or until the vegetables and pasta are tender. Check the seasoning before serving, then sprinkle the soup with grated Parmesan.

Trim the celery

Trim the celery leaves and root end. Make a shallow cut at the end with a serrated knife and pull down the tough outer strings to remove them.

Prepare the cabbage

Cut the cabbage into quarters and remove the core at the bases. Remove the thick central rib from each leaf before cutting it into strips.

Top, tail, and slice the French beans

1 Using your fingers, gently break off the top and tail end of each bean. They should snap off quite easily.

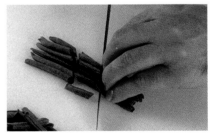

2 Line up several beans together in a tight bunch. Slice diagonally across into equal-sized pieces.

Clam Chowder

Fresh clams and fresh cobs of corn make this chowder rather special. However, if you want to make it in a hurry, it's fine to use canned clams and frozen or canned sweetcorn. Chunks of warm garlic bread make a great accompaniment.

Ingredients

Serves 4

350g (12oz) fresh clams, cleaned, or 280g can baby clams in brine, drained
1 corn cob or 100g (3½oz) sweetcorn kernels, thawed if frozen
75g (2½oz) smoked streaky bacon rashers, rinds removed, chopped
1 onion, peeled and finely chopped
20g (¾oz) butter
20g (¾oz) plain flour
400ml (14fl oz) hot milk
300g (10oz) potatoes, peeled and diced
salt and freshly ground black pepper
150ml (5fl oz) double cream

PER SERVING

Calories: 374
Saturated fat: 12g
Unsaturated fat: 9g
Sodium: 785mg

Method

1 If using fresh clams, soak them for at least 1 hour in cold salted water (4 tablespoons salt to 1 litre/1¾ pints water), drain well, then scrub the shells as shown below. Steam in a covered pan for about 5 minutes until fully open. When cooled, remove the clams from their shells and set aside. If using fresh sweetcorn, cut the kernels off the cobs as shown below.

2 Heat a large pan over a low heat for 30 seconds, add the bacon and onion and cook for 5 minutes, stirring. Add the butter, stir until melted, then sprinkle in the flour and stir to mix.

3 Remove the pan from the heat and gradually stir in the hot milk. Return the pan to a low heat and continue stirring until the mixture thickens and bubbles.

4 Add the potatoes, salt and pepper, and fresh sweetcorn, if using, and cook for 10–15 minutes, or until the potatoes are tender. Add the cream and bring back to a simmer. If using frozen or tinned sweetcorn, add it at the same time as the cream.

5 Add the clams to the soup and heat through gently. Do not let the soup boil, as this will toughen the clams. Check the seasoning before serving.

Clean the clams

After soaking the clams, scrub the shells with a stiff brush under cold running water to remove any sand and grit. Discard any open clams or clams with broken shells.

Dehusk the sweetcorn

Remove the husk, stalk, and silky threads. Hold the corn cob upright on a cutting board and, using a chef's knife, slice straight down the sides to cut the kernels off the cob.

First Courses

Master Recipe

Cheese Soufflés

Making a soufflé is not difficult, just a little fiddly. The key is to make a good cheese sauce (or "base") for flavour, whisk the egg whites to the right consistency for light, airy volume, and keep an eye on timing. Individual soufflés make an exciting first course, or baked in one larger dish, a soufflé is ideal for supper served with salad.

 Serves 6   **Prep** 15 mins   ⏱ **Cook** 35–50 mins

Ingredients

300ml (10fl oz) milk
45g (1½oz) butter, plus extra
   for greasing
45g (1½oz) plain flour
150g (5½oz) strong Cheddar
   cheese, grated
1 tsp Dijon mustard
salt and freshly ground
   black pepper
4 large eggs

Special equipment

6 x 150ml (5fl oz) ramekins or,
to make 1 large soufflé, a 600ml
(1 pint) soufflé dish

PER SERVING

Calories: 409
Saturated fat: 18g
Unsaturated fat: 12g
Sodium: 496mg

Cook's notes

Getting the timing right

Soufflés deflate soon after you remove them from the oven, so ensure your guests are seated in good time and serve immediately.

Prepare ahead

You can make the soufflé base up to 3 hours ahead. However, you'll need to whisk the egg whites and finish the soufflé just before baking and serve straight from the oven.

Make the soufflé base

 Prep 5 mins   ⏱ **Cook** 20 mins

KEY to SUCCESS Do not let the butter or flour brown. The flour-butter mixture ("roux") should be a pale gold colour.

1 Heat the milk in a small pan until just boiling. In another pan, melt the butter over a medium heat, add the flour, and whisk until well mixed.

2 Remove the pan from the heat and gradually whisk in the hot milk. Add a little to start with and mix well until smooth, then add the rest.

3 Return the pan to a medium heat. Continue whisking vigorously with a hand whisk until the sauce is boiling and thickened. It is important to keep whisking so the mixture does not form lumps.

4 When you feel the sauce thickening, remove the pan from the heat and add the grated cheese, stirring until it has melted. Add the mustard, salt, and pepper. Leave the sauce to cool a little.

KEY to SUCCESS As with all cheese sauces, add cheese off the heat so that it melts but does not overcook.

KEY to SUCCESS Make sure there is no yolk mixed into the white or the white will not whisk to its full volume.

KEY to SUCCESS The sauce should be lukewarm or cooler before you add the egg whites.

5 Separate the egg yolks from the egg whites. Crack each egg in half and tip the contents between the two shells, allowing the whites to slide through into the bowl beneath while the yolks stay in the shells.

6 Whisk the egg yolks into the hot sauce, one yolk at a time, whisking thoroughly after each addition until the mixture is completely smooth. Set the mixture aside to cool before adding the egg whites (see overleaf).

Finish and bake the soufflés

Prep 10 mins   **Cook** 15–30 mins

1 Preheat the oven to 180°C (fan 160°C/350°F/Gas 4) and put a baking tray on the middle shelf. Brush the ramekin insides with soft butter.

KEY to SUCCESS Before you whisk egg whites, make sure both the bowl and the whisk are clean and grease-free.

2 Whisk the egg whites in a large bowl with a balloon whisk or electric mixer on a high setting until fluffy, stiff, and resembling clouds.

3 Add 2 heaped tablespoons of the egg whites into the cooled sauce and beat well with the whisk to slacken the mixture.

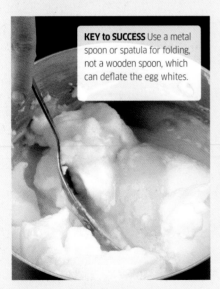

KEY to SUCCESS Use a metal spoon or spatula for folding, not a wooden spoon, which can deflate the egg whites.

4 Gently fold in the rest of the egg whites using a figure-of-eight motion, cutting through the mixture, then turning it over until well blended.

5 Spoon the mixture to the top of the ramekins and level off. Run a thumb nail around the inside rim to prevent the soufflé catching the sides.

KEY to SUCCESS Do not open the oven door while the soufflés are cooking or they are likely to "sink".

6 Place the ramekins on the baking tray. Bake for 15–20 minutes (25–30 for a larger dish), or until risen and just starting to go golden brown.

"Soufflés make a perfect first course: beautifully light and delicate, they never fail to impress."

Bruschetta with Goat's Cheese and Onion Marmalade

Bruschetta make a good substantial starter or lunchtime snack. Use the recipe for Onion Marmalade on pp142-43, but add another 2 teaspoons balsamic vinegar and 1 tablespoon sugar: the goat's cheese benefits from the extra sweetness.

Ingredients

Makes 4

2 tsp extra virgin olive oil,
    plus extra for drizzling
1 small garlic clove, peeled and finely
    chopped
4 diagonal slices of ciabatta
3 tbsp onion marmalade (see above)
125g (4½oz) goat's cheese, ideally
    log-shaped
rocket leaves, to serve
freshly ground black pepper
balsamic vinegar, to drizzle

PER SERVING

Calories: 251
Saturated fat: 7g
Unsaturated fat: 8g
Sodium: 349mg

Method

1 Preheat the grill to its highest setting. In a small bowl, mix the oil with the garlic. Place the ciabatta slices on a baking sheet and toast them on one side only under the grill, then remove them from the heat, turn the bread over, and brush the untoasted side with the garlic oil.

2 Spread a thick layer of onion marmalade over each slice of bread, on top of the garlic oil. Cut the goat's cheese into 8 slices, about 1cm (½in) thick, and lay 2 slices, overlapping, on each slice of bread.

3 Put the bread slices back under the grill, quite close to the heat, for about 3 minutes, or until the cheese is just starting to bubble and turn a lovely golden brown colour. Do not over-cook; they want to be just crisp.

4 Scatter a few rocket leaves on a serving platter, lay the bruschetta on top, season with pepper, and drizzle with the olive oil and a few drops of balsamic vinegar.

The easy way to peel and chop garlic

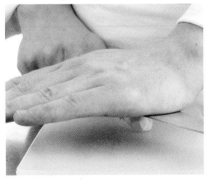

1 Place the garlic clove on a chopping board. Set the flat side of a knife on top of the clove and press down with your palm; this will loosen the skin.

2 Use a knife or your fingers to peel off the skin and discard. Again, set the flat side of the knife on top of the clove and press to flatten slightly.

3 Slice the flattened clove into thin slivers lengthways, then cut across. Gather the pieces into a pile and chop again for finer dice.

Chargrilled Asparagus with Quick Hollandaise

It is usual to simply boil asparagus for dipping into this rich, creamy sauce, but chargrilling adds a unique flavour. When making this quick version of hollandaise, I've found that heating the blender first allows the sauce to thicken more easily.

Ingredients

Serves 4

550-600g (1¼-1lb 5oz)
    asparagus, trimmed
olive oil, for brushing
salt and freshly ground black pepper
lemon wedges, to serve

FOR THE QUICK HOLLANDAISE

1 tbsp lemon juice
1 tbsp white wine vinegar
3 large egg yolks (room temperature)
175g (6oz) unsalted butter, melted

PER SERVING

Calories: 456
Saturated fat: 25g
Unsaturated fat: 21g
Sodium: 273mg

Method

1 Lay the asparagus in a large shallow frying pan or sauté pan. Pour over enough boiling water from a kettle to just cover it, then bring back to the boil and simmer gently for 2–3 minutes, until it turns bright green but is still fairly firm. Drain well and pat dry. Set aside to cool.

2 Meanwhile, make the quick hollandaise: three-quarters fill a food processor or blender with hot water from the kettle and pulse or process briefly to warm the bowl. Pour the water away and dry the bowl.

3 Put the lemon juice and vinegar into the food processor or blender, drop in the egg yolks and pulse or process briefly. With the machine running, gradually pour in the melted butter, a little at a time. Keep slowly adding the butter, working until the mixture is thick and creamy. Discard any milky liquid that is in the bottom of the pan. Season to taste.

4 Brush the asparagus all over with olive oil. Preheat a ridged cast-iron chargrill pan, and when very hot, lay the asparagus on the pan and grill for about 2 minutes, turning once, until griddle marks appear and the asparagus is tender but still with a bite. Do this in batches if necessary. Season and serve with the hollandaise and lemon wedges.

Trim the asparagus

With a sharp chef's knife, cut the hard, woody ends from the asparagus spears and discard. Alternatively, snap the bottoms of the spears.

How to separate an egg

1 Tap the middle of an egg sharply against a bowl rim. Prise the shell apart with your thumbs. Some of the white will escape into the bowl.

2 Shift the yolk between the shell halves, letting the white fall into the bowl. Place the yolk into another bowl and leave to reach room temperature.

Chicken Liver and Aubergine Pâté

Adding some aubergine to a liver pâté makes it much lighter and less calorific.
It gives a more silky-smooth texture too. Serve the pâté in individual pots or one
larger dish with toast, and if you have any left over, try it as a spread in sandwiches.

Ingredients

Serves 4

175g (6oz) chicken livers,
  thawed if frozen
85g (3oz) butter (room temperature)
1 shallot, peeled and finely chopped
1 small aubergine, about 175g (6oz),
  peeled and diced
85g (3oz) full-fat cream cheese
1 tsp lemon juice
1 tsp soy sauce
1 tbsp chopped fresh parsley,
  plus extra to garnish
freshly grated nutmeg
salt and freshly ground black pepper

PER SERVING

Calories: 215
Saturated fat: 10.5g
Unsaturated fat: 7g
Sodium: 305mg

Method

1 Rinse the chicken livers and drain well in a colander for about
10 minutes. Place them on a double thickness of kitchen paper
to absorb excess liquid. Trim the livers as shown below.

2 Melt 45g (1½oz) of the butter in a large non-stick frying pan and sauté
the chicken livers until cooked through. Remove from the pan with
a slotted spoon, transfer to a plate, and set aside. Put the shallot in the
pan and fry for about 2 minutes, or until softened.

3 Add another 30g (1oz) butter to the pan with the shallot, let it melt,
then tip in the diced aubergine and fry briskly for a few minutes until
well softened. Set aside to cool.

4 Purée the cooled aubergine mixture and chicken livers in a food
processor until smooth. Add the remaining butter, cream cheese,
lemon juice, soy sauce, and parsley, and purée again until evenly blended.
Season well to taste with nutmeg, salt, and pepper.

5 Divide the mixture between 4 small ramekins, smooth the tops,
and chill the pâté in the fridge before serving. Garnish with a light
sprinkling of chopped parsley.

Trim the chicken livers

Using a paring knife, trim the chicken
livers. Cut away any white sinew and
greenish patches.

Grate the nutmeg finely

Rub the whole nutmeg across the
surface of a microplane grater or
special nutmeg grater (see p26).

Moules Marinière

You can buy mussels all year round, but early autumn to mid-spring is best. Make sure they are really fresh. It's best to use fresh fish stock if possible, but if you don't have any, a fish stock cube dissolved in boiling water will be absolutely fine.

Ingredients

Serves 4

2kg (4½lb) live mussels, cleaned
2 tbsp olive oil
6 spring onions, trimmed and
    finely chopped
4 celery sticks, trimmed and
    finely chopped
2 garlic cloves, peeled and crushed
300ml (10fl oz) dry white wine
1 bouquet garni (see p136)
salt and freshly ground black pepper
300ml (10fl oz) hot fish stock
generous knob of butter
4 tbsp chopped fresh parsley

PER SERVING

Calories: 544
Saturated fat: 6g
Unsaturated fat: 14g
Sodium: 1582mg

Method

1 First prepare the mussels as shown on p200. Discard any open mussels or those with broken shells. Set aside.

2 Heat the oil in a large pan, add the vegetables and garlic, and fry over a medium heat for about 5 minutes, or until softened, stirring.

3 Add the wine, bouquet garni, mussels, and salt and pepper. Cover the pan and cook over a high heat for about 5 minutes, or until the mussels are open, shaking the pan occasionally.

4 Lift out the mussels and put them into 4 warmed soup plates, discarding any that are not open. Keep warm.

5 Remove the bouquet garni, add the stock to the pan, and boil for 3–4 minutes until the liquid has reduced and thickened a little. Add the butter and whisk until melted, then the parsley. Check the seasoning and pour the sauce over the mussels.

How I make fresh fish stock

1 Put the rinsed heads, bones, and skin of 3 fish into a large pan, cutting them up with a knife to fit if necessary. Use salmon or white fish, not dark, oily varieties such as mackerel or herring.

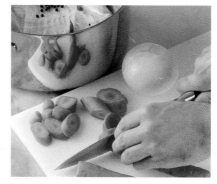

2 Coarsely chop 3 carrots, 2 onions, 2 leeks, and 1 celery stick and add to the pan with parsley and thyme sprigs, and peppercorns. Completely cover with cold water. Bring to the boil.

3 Skim the scum off the surface, lower the heat, and simmer for 30 minutes. Remove from the heat and strain into a large bowl. Keeps for 2 days in the fridge and 6 months in the freezer.

Mary's Secrets of Success

First Courses

1 **When choosing a first course**, look at your menu as a whole and provide a balance of flavours and textures without repetition. If you're serving a meaty main course, offer a fish or vegetarian starter for contrast, and vice versa.

Spiced Scallops and Pancetta, pp62–63

2 **Bear in mind** a first course should stimulate the taste buds rather than spoil the appetite. Keep starters small and not over rich, to leave guests wanting more.

Chargrilled Asparagus with Quick Hollandaise, pp54–55

3 **If you're pushed for time** or have a complicated main course planned, make a first course you can prepare ahead. Remember, most hot dishes require last-minute work, even if they're prepared in advance.

4 **Present your first courses beautifully:** decorate dishes that are not naturally bright in colour with fresh herbs or other colourful garnishes.

5 For informal occasions, I often lay out canapés on a platter, which I pass around with drinks, rather than serving a first course at the table.

6 Consider providing a selection of starters as a main meal, mezze style, instead of the more traditional three courses. This particularly suits people who live in a small space without a dining table.

7 Meticulous planning is the key to success when you're entertaining. If you're serving a hot first course, have everything you need to hand before you start, such as oven gloves, utensils, and a timer.

8 When serving a hot first course, to speed things along I arrange the garnish on the individual plates in advance, then add the hot food and serve straight away.

9 Assemble your guests before doing any last-minute cooking or reheating, otherwise the food may get cold.

10 If I'm serving a cold starter, I like to put the plates in position at each place setting before calling the guests in to eat – it's more welcoming that way. Make sure you keep the doors shut if you have a cat or a dog!

Cheese Soufflés, pp48–51

Spiced Scallops and Pancetta

Serving scallops always makes a meal rather special. Here they are combined with a touch of mild Asian spice mix and pancetta. I've used the large, plump "king" scallops as they're so succulent and delicious. Serve over Chinese egg noodles.

Ingredients

Serves 4

2 large carrots, peeled
6 spring onions, trimmed
50g (1¾oz) pancetta
1 tbsp sunflower oil
200g (7oz) shelled scallops, trimmed
   and sliced if necessary
250ml (9fl oz) coconut milk
1 tsp caster sugar
salt
75g (2½oz) dried medium Chinese egg
   noodles, soaked, to serve (see p116)
fresh coriander leaves, to garnish

FOR THE SPICE MIX

3 garlic cloves, peeled and crushed
2.5cm (1in) piece of fresh root ginger,
   peeled and chopped
2 tsp mild curry powder
2 tbsp sunflower oil

PER SERVING

Calories: 368
Saturated fat: 9g
Unsaturated fat: 12g
Sodium: 312mg

BUYING AND USING SCALLOPS

Scallops are usually sold without their shells. They should have a sweet, fresh smell and plump, creamy flesh. You can't always buy scallops with their orange coral still attached, but if you can, leave them on to serve as an extra delicacy. Scallops cook in 3–4 minutes, so do not exceed this time or they will be rubbery.

Method

1 First make the spice mix: place all the ingredients for the mix in a food processor fitted with the metal blade and process until smooth. Alternatively, pound in a pestle and mortar.

2 Slice the carrots into thin sticks and slice the spring onions diagonally. Cut the pancetta into small cubes the size of a pea.

3 Heat a non-stick sauté pan or wok over a high heat for 1–2 minutes until very hot. Add the oil and heat until it just begins to smoke. Fry the pancetta for 1 minute.

4 Reduce the heat to medium, add the carrots and stir-fry for 1 minute. Add the spice mix and stir-fry for 2 minutes. Add the scallops and spring onions and stir-fry over a high heat for about 3 minutes.

5 Add the coconut milk, sugar, and salt. Stir and heat until bubbling. To serve, pour the scallop and pancetta mixture over Chinese egg noodles and garnish with coriander leaves.

Trim and slice the scallops

1 Using sharp kitchen scissors, cut off and discard the crescent-shaped muscle on the side of the white body of the scallop.

2 Large scallops cook best if sliced. Using a chef's knife, slice through into rounds. Small "queen" scallops can be left whole.

Garlic Prawns with Tomato Sauce

This makes a smart first course and adds variety to the menu if you're planning a meaty main course. It's best to buy tiger prawns for this dish, as their size is more impressive and they're so juicy and flavoursome.

Ingredients

Serves 4

16–20 tiger prawns, peeled
and deveined (ideally raw)
5 tbsp olive oil
3 garlic cloves, peeled and crushed
salt and freshly ground black pepper
250ml (9fl oz) tomato passata
juice of ½ lemon
1 tsp caster sugar
100g (3½oz) long-grain rice, boiled,
to serve (see p120)
3 tbsp coarsely chopped fresh
parsley, to garnish
coarsely grated zest of 1 lemon,
to garnish

PER SERVING

Calories: 340
Saturated fat: 3g
Unsaturated fat: 16g
Sodium: 416mg

BUYING AND USING PRAWNS

Tiger prawns are available either whole with their shells on, or with their heads removed (in which case they are often called prawn tails). If using whole prawns, don't discard the shells; they make a flavourful stock (see fish stock, p58, and replace the fish trimmings with the prawn shells). If using cooked prawns, just heat them through for a minute or two in the passata.

Method

1 Place the prawns in a large bowl with the oil, garlic, and salt and pepper. Toss well to mix.

2 Meanwhile, heat a large non-stick sauté pan over a high heat for 2 minutes. Add the raw prawns with the oil and garlic and stir for 2 minutes, or until pink. Reduce the heat to medium and add the passata, lemon juice, and sugar. Cook, stirring, for 3–4 minutes. Check seasoning.

3 Serve the prawns over long-grain rice and garnish with parsley and lemon zest.

Peel and devein the prawns

1 If the head is still on the prawn, pinch it between your fingers and pull it from the body to leave just the fleshy tail end intact.

2 Peel the shell from the body with your fingers, working down from the head. When you reach the tail, pull the meat out of the shell.

3 If the prawn is large, remove the dark vein, or intestinal tract: make a shallow cut along the back of the prawn with a paring knife to reveal it.

4 Pick out the end of the vein with the tip of the knife; gently pull it out, starting from the head end and working down. Discard the vein.

Prawn Cocktail

Serving glasses that show off the tiered presentation are ideal for this classic first course. You can make the sauce 3 days ahead and assemble the dish 4 hours ahead. For a lighter sauce, use light mayonnaise and half-fat crème fraîche or plain yogurt.

Ingredients

Serves 4

225g (8oz) cooked, peeled North
    Atlantic prawns, drained and
    patted dry
handful of watercress
1 Little Gem lettuce
85g (3oz) piece of cucumber
paprika, for dusting
lime wedges, to serve

FOR THE SAUCE

6 tbsp mayonnaise
3 tbsp crème fraîche
2 tbsp tomato ketchup
1½–2 tbsp creamed horseradish
    sauce (see p152)
1 tsp tomato purée
½ tsp Worcestershire sauce
a few drops of Tabasco sauce
about 1 tbsp lemon juice
salt and freshly ground black pepper

PER SERVING

Calories: 283
Saturated fat: 6g
Unsaturated fat: 17g
Sodium: 654mg

Method

1 Make the Marie Rose sauce: mix the mayonnaise, crème fraîche, ketchup, horseradish sauce, tomato purée, Worcestershire sauce, Tabasco, and lemon juice together in a bowl. Add salt and pepper. Taste and adjust the seasoning, adding more horseradish sauce and lemon juice, if needed.

2 Take 4 serving glasses and put a few peeled prawns in the bottom of each. Spoon over a little of the sauce.

3 Trim off any long or thick stems from the watercress, shred the lettuce, and dice the cucumber. Mix the watercress leaves with the lettuce and cucumber. Season with pepper.

4 Divide the greenery between the glasses, then top each with the remaining prawns.

5 Spoon the rest of the sauce over the prawns, dust with paprika, and serve with lime wedges.

VARIATION Prawn and Avocado Cocktail Toss 1 small, ripe, diced avocado in with the lettuce mixture.

Make the Marie Rose sauce

Put all the ingredients for the sauce in a small bowl and whisk with a fork or stir with a spoon to combine. It should be both piquant and creamy.

Eggs

Classic French Omelette

Nothing could be simpler or quicker to prepare than an omelette: with just a few basic ingredients you can whip up a delicious impromptu meal. The classic French omelette is plain, but the possibilities for flavourings and fillings are endless. Here, I've added the French combination of aromatic herbs, known as *fines herbes*.

 Serves 1   **Prep** 3 mins   **Cook** No more than 1¼–1½ mins

Ingredients

2 large eggs
1 tbsp chopped fresh herbs, such as chives, parsley, tarragon, and chervil (if available)
1 tbsp water
salt and freshly ground black pepper
walnut-size knob of butter

Special equipment
A non-stick omelette pan, 18–20cm (7–8in) across, with curved sides

PER SERVING
Calories: 281
Saturated fat: 10g
Unsaturated fat: 10g
Sodium: 327mg

Cook's notes

Use the right size pan
An omelette pan 18–20cm (7–8in) across is the ideal size for a 2- or 3-egg omelette. Too large a pan and you'll have a thin, dry omelette; too small, and it will be leathery beneath and uncooked on top.

Fines herbes
This classic herb mixture contains equal quantities of chives, chervil, parsley, and tarragon.

Eat straightaway
An omelette must be eaten as soon as it is cooked. It quickly goes cold and the texture becomes rubbery.

Prepare the ingredients

 **Prep** 3 mins

KEY to SUCCESS Stir the eggs gently with a fork: do not over-beat, as this makes the omelette rubbery.

Crack the eggs into a bowl, then add the chopped fresh herbs, water, and salt and pepper. Stir gently with a fork, just enough to break up the yolks and whites.

Cook the omelette

🕐 **Cook** 1¼–1½ mins

> **KEY to SUCCESS** Preheat the pan over a high heat until piping hot so the omelette will cook very rapidly.

1 Heat the pan over a high heat for about 30 seconds, or until very hot. Add the butter: it will quickly start to foam. Tilt the pan so the butter coats the base.

2 As soon as the butter has melted and stopped foaming (the sizzling sound will subside), pour in the egg and herb mixture. Tilt the pan to spread the egg over the base.

3 After about 10 seconds, use a wooden spatula to begin to pull the cooked egg from the edge towards the centre, allowing the liquid egg to flow into the space.

Eggs

KEY to SUCCESS For variety, omit the herbs and add chopped cooked ham or grated cheese (Cheddar, Gruyère, or Stilton) at this stage.

4 Continue for about 1–1¼ minutes, until the omelette holds together and there is not enough liquid to flow into the spaces. At this stage it will still be runny on top.

5 Tilt the omelette pan to one side and use the spatula to fold the omelette over. Jiggle the pan gently so that the omelette slides to the edge.

KEY to SUCCESS The way you serve the omelette is up to you. Half-folded like this is easiest, but you could also try folding in thirds, like an envelope, with the two edges tucked underneath.

6 Bring a plate up to the pan. Tip the pan further so the omelette rolls over and falls onto the plate. Serve straightaway.

"A simple omelette is my idea of the perfect mid-week lunch, being super-speedy to cook, light, and nutritious."

The Ultimate Soft-boiled Egg

Boiled eggs are among the healthiest ways of eating eggs, as you don't use any butter or oil. I recommend buying free-range eggs for boiling – you'll find the yolks are a brighter colour and they have more flavour.

Ingredients

Serves 2

2 large eggs
salt and freshly ground black pepper
toast, to serve

PER SERVING

Calories: 100
Saturated fat: 2g
Unsaturated fat: 5.5g
Sodium: 98mg

Method

1 Take the eggs out of the fridge at least 30 minutes before cooking; the shells will crack in hot water if the eggs are very cold.

2 Using a pin, make a tiny hole about 1cm (½in) deep in the rounded end of the shell, to allow the steam to escape. Otherwise, pressure can build up during the boiling process and cause cracking. Also, breaking the seal between the membrane and the egg white tends to make the egg a little easier to peel.

3 Place a small pan of water on the hob (about two-thirds full) and bring it to the boil. If you use a large pan to boil several eggs, the eggs can crash into each other and the shells may crack.

4 Using a slotted spoon, gently lower the eggs into the pan, one at a time. Bring the water to the boil again, then lower the heat to a gentle simmer and set a timer for 4 minutes for a set white and a runny yolk.

5 When the time is up, remove the eggs with a slotted spoon and slice across the top with a knife. The eggs will have a runny yolk. Sprinkle with salt and pepper to taste, and serve with toast.

How I test an egg for freshness

FRESH To test if an egg is fresh, gently drop it into a glass of cold water. If it is really fresh it will lie horizontally at the bottom of the glass.

BORDERLINE If, after settling, the egg begins to rise in the water at one end, it is not completely fresh but it is fine to use it.

STALE If the egg bobs up towards the surface of the water in a vertical position, it means the egg is stale and should be discarded.

Scrambled Eggs

This is my Sunday night supper. To make the texture wonderfully creamy, cook the eggs as slowly as possible. For a special occasion, replace the milk with single cream and serve the eggs with 200g (7oz) sliced smoked salmon alongside.

Ingredients

Serves 4

15g (½oz) butter
8 large eggs
salt and freshly ground black pepper
4 tbsp milk

PER SERVING

Calories: 238
Saturated fat: 6.5g
Unsaturated fat: 12.5g
Sodium: 227mg

Method

1 Melt the butter in a 20cm (8in) non-stick pan, such as a milk or sauté pan, over a low heat. If the pan is not non-stick, there is a risk that the eggs will stick and burn on the bottom.

2 Meanwhile, crack the eggs into a bowl, season with salt and pepper, and beat with a whisk or fork. Add the milk, then beat again until the eggs and milk are thoroughly blended.

3 When the butter in the pan has melted, pour in the egg and milk mixture and cook over an extremely low heat for about 3 minutes, stirring all the time.

4 When the eggs are almost set, remove the pan from the heat, stir for 1 more minute, then serve at once, with a grinding of pepper over the top. Do not overcook – scrambled eggs should be creamy, not set and fried.

VARIATION Scrambled Eggs with Chives Add 1 tablespoon fresh chopped chives to the scrambled egg mixture in step 2.

How to make scrambled eggs silky-smooth

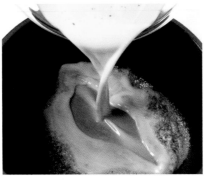

1 Make very light, fast movements with a whisk or fork until the seasoned eggs and milk are one consistency.

2 Wait until the butter is foaming before adding the eggs. Keep the heat very low; watch and stir constantly.

3 If the eggs are setting too quickly, take the pan off the heat, stir, and replace. The eggs must remain moist.

Mary's Secrets of Success

Eggs

1 **When buying eggs,** always check them carefully, ensuring they're fresh and avoiding any with cracked shells.

2 **I store my eggs in the fridge** as they last a lot longer. I keep them in the carton and away from strong foods, so they don't absorb flavours and odours through their shells.

3 **It's best to store eggs** with their pointed ends facing downwards. This ensures that the yolk remains centred in the white and keeps eggs fresh for longer.

4 **Always use eggs by their "best before" date.** This is important for safety; also, stale eggs have flat yolks and watery whites, which spoil both texture and taste.

5 **If whisking egg whites,** take eggs out of the fridge several hours in advance, to bring them to room temperature – this way, you get more volume.

Classic French Omelette, pp70–73

6 **For soft-boiling or hard-boiling,** use eggs at room temperature, because they're less likely to crack.

7 **Look out for the "British Lion" mark** on eggs, as it denotes the birds have been vaccinated against salmonella.

Italian Herb Frittata, pp82–83

The Ultimate Soft-boiled Egg, pp74–75

8 **When making custard or adding eggs to sauces,** it helps to stir a little hot liquid into beaten eggs first; this prevents the eggs from curdling when they're added to more hot liquid.

9 **I freeze leftover yolks or whites,** adding a little salt or sugar to the yolks, depending on what I'm going to use them for. There's no need to add anything to the whites. Just remember to label the container.

10 **To prevent salmonella poisoning,** always wash hands really well after dealing with raw egg. Avoid serving raw, runny, or softly set eggs to babies, young children, the sick, and the elderly.

Eggs Benedict, pp80–81

Eggs Benedict

Ideal for a special breakfast or informal lunch, this is a classic – but for a variation, or to suit vegetarians, you can serve the egg on a bed of wilted, buttered spinach. Don't let the hollandaise get too hot while cooking, or it will become too thick.

Ingredients

Serves 4

2 muffins, halved
4 eggs
butter, for spreading
4 slices good-quality ham

FOR THE HOLLANDAISE SAUCE

2 tsp lemon juice
2 tsp white wine vinegar
2 large egg yolks (room temperature)
125g (4½oz) unsalted butter, melted
salt and freshly ground black pepper

PER SERVING

Calories: 468
Saturated fat: 20g
Unsaturated fat: 18g
Sodium: 685mg

Method

1 First make the hollandaise sauce as shown below. Add only clear melted butter to the sauce, and discard any milky liquid that has collected on the bottom of the pan. Season the sauce and keep warm.

2 Toast the cut sides of the muffin halves under a hot grill and keep warm. Poach the eggs as shown below.

3 Butter the muffin halves and place on warmed plates. Lay a slice of ham on top of each muffin half, then a poached egg. Top each with a spoonful of the hollandaise sauce.

Poach the eggs to perfection

1 Crack an egg onto a small plate, then slide it into gently simmering salted water. Reduce the heat to low. Poach only 1 or 2 eggs at a time.

2 Swirl water around the edges to give neat shapes. Simmer gently for about 3 minutes until the white is opaque. Lift out with a slotted spoon and drain.

Make a rich, creamy hollandaise sauce

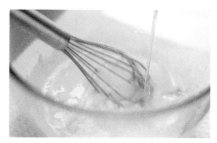

1 Put the lemon juice and vinegar into a medium heatproof bowl. Tip in the egg yolks and whisk with a balloon whisk until light and frothy.

2 Place the bowl over a pan containing simmering water. Whisk for 2 minutes, or until the mixture thickens enough to leave a trail when the whisk is lifted.

3 Remove from the heat and gradually pour in the melted butter, a little at a time, whisking constantly. Whisk until the sauce is thick, glossy, and smooth.

Italian Herb Frittata

A frittata is a baked omelette. Take care not to over-bake it or it will become tough. If you don't have an omelette pan you can use a 23cm (9in) round flameproof, ovenproof dish instead.

Ingredients

Serves 4

8 large eggs
150ml (5fl oz) single cream
50g (1¾oz) Cheddar cheese, grated
25g (scant 1oz) Parmesan cheese, grated
1 tbsp chopped fresh parsley
1 tbsp snipped fresh chives
salt and freshly ground black pepper
2 tbsp olive oil

PER SERVING

Calories: 400
Saturated fat: 13g
Unsaturated fat: 19g
Sodium: 339mg

Method

1 Preheat the oven to 180°C (fan 160°C/350°F/Gas 4). In a large bowl, beat the eggs with the cream, both cheeses, herbs, and salt and pepper.

2 Heat the oil in a 23cm (9in) oven-safe, non-stick omelette pan over a medium heat until hot. Pour in the egg mixture and shake the pan a little to spread the ingredients evenly.

3 Transfer the pan to the oven and bake for 20 minutes, or until the omelette is just set in the centre.

4 Hold a warmed plate upside-down over the pan and turn the two over together so that the omelette inverts onto the plate. Serve hot or warm.

VARIATION Sun-blushed Tomato and Basil Frittata Replace the parsley and chives with 50g (1¾oz) sunblushed tomatoes and 1 tablespoon shredded basil leaves.

SERVING FRITTATA

Frittatas are very versatile. They can be served hot or cold, as a simple main course with salad, or sliced up into smaller pieces and served with drinks. Vegetarian options are shown here, but they can also contain meat, such as ham or cooked sausage. They are a great way to use up any leftovers.

Chop the parsley

For robust herbs, such as parsley, thyme, and rosemary, strip the leaves from the stalks. Hold the tip of the knife and chop the leaves by rocking the blade up and down on the board.

Snip the chives

Chives have hollow stems, so they are easier to snip with a pair of kitchen scissors than they are to chop with a knife. Hold a small bunch over a bowl and snip them finely.

"I always keep a carton of eggs in the fridge. As well as making a delicious light meal in their own right, they're used in so many recipes to thicken, enrich, lighten, bind, and glaze."

Egg Mayonnaise with Herbs

This is a lower-fat version of a classic recipe. It is good as a first course, or as a summer salad at lunchtime with a green salad on the side. You can prepare the sauce up to 3 hours ahead and keep it in the fridge.

Ingredients

Serves 4

6 large eggs
60–70g (2–2½oz) rocket leaves
1–2 tbsp French dressing (see p236)

FOR THE SAUCE

100ml (3½fl oz) low-fat crème fraîche
   or low-fat plain yogurt
100ml (3½fl oz) light mayonnaise
1 tbsp lemon juice
½ tsp caster sugar
1 tbsp each finely chopped fresh
   parsley, mint, basil, and tarragon
salt and freshly ground black pepper

PER SERVING

Calories: 364
Saturated fat: 5g
Unsaturated fat: 24g
Sodium 643mg

Method

1 First make the sauce: mix together all the sauce ingredients, then taste to check the seasoning. Cover and chill.

2 Hard-boil, peel, and cool the eggs as shown below, then drain and dry them. Do not cook the eggs for any longer than 10 minutes, or a greenish black ring will form around the yolk.

3 Place a cooked egg on a chopping board and use a sharp knife to slice it in half lengthways. Repeat for the remaining eggs.

4 Just before serving, arrange the rocket leaves on a serving plate and spoon the French dressing evenly over them.

5 Place the egg halves, cut-side up in a clover-leaf pattern, on top of the rocket. Spoon the sauce over them. Serve 3 egg halves per person.

VARIATION Curried Eggs Omit the herbs and add 2 tablespoons mango chutney and 1 tablespoon curry powder.

BOILING EGGS

Although we talk about boiling eggs, in actual fact they must be simmered rather than boiled. This applies to both soft-boiled eggs (when the whites are set and the yolks runny) and hard-boiled eggs (when both the whites and the yolks are set). After bringing the water to the boil, always turn the heat down so they can simmer gently.

Hard-boil and shell the eggs

1 Follow the instructions for soft-boiled eggs (see p74), but simmer for 10 minutes. Lift out the eggs with a slotted spoon and plunge them into a bowl of cold water to stop them cooking.

2 When the eggs are cool enough to hold, crack the shells and peel them. Both the yolks and whites will be set. Put the eggs in cold water for at least 5 minutes until cool. Drain and dry.

Quiche Lorraine

A classic French quiche is a great stand-by for lunch or supper and is always best eaten hot or warm. Baking the pastry "blind" first, without the filling, ensures that the pastry case is cooked through so it doesn't get a soggy bottom.

Ingredients

Serves 8

175g (6oz) unsmoked streaky
   bacon rashers, rinds removed,
   cut into strips
1 onion, peeled and chopped
125g (4½oz) Gruyère cheese, grated
2 large eggs
250ml (9fl oz) single cream
salt and freshly ground black pepper

FOR THE PASTRY

175g (6oz) plain flour, plus extra
   for dusting
85g (3oz) hard block margarine or
   chilled butter, cut into cubes

PER SERVING

Calories: 371
Saturated fat: 13g
Unsaturated fat: 12.5g
Sodium: 506mg

Method

1 First make the pastry: tip the flour into a large mixing bowl. Add the margarine or butter and rub in gently with the fingertips until the mixture resembles fine breadcrumbs (see p272). Add 3 tablespoons cold water until the pastry comes together in a ball.

2 Roll out the dough on a lightly floured surface and use it to line a 20cm (8in) loose-bottomed flan tin (see pp254–55). Ideally, use a fluted tin.

3 Chill in the fridge for 30 minutes. Meanwhile, preheat the oven to 220°C (fan 200°C/425°F/Gas 7). Blind bake the pastry case (see p274).

4 Reduce the oven temperature to 180°C (fan 160°C/350°F/Gas 4). Crisp the bacon in a sauté pan over a medium heat for 10 minutes, as shown below. Transfer to the cooled pastry case with a slotted spoon. Leave the juices in the pan.

5 Place the onion in the pan and cook over a medium heat for 8 minutes, or until golden. Add to the quiche and top with the cheese.

6 In a bowl, combine the eggs, cream, salt, and pepper, then pour into the quiche. Bake for 25–30 minutes until golden and just set. Be careful not to overcook the quiche, or the filling will become tough and full of holes.

How to fry bacon the healthier way

1 Remove the rinds. Stack the bacon rashers on a chopping board and cut them crossways into 5mm (¼in) strips.

2 Place the bacon into a frying pan (without oil or butter) and fry, stirring occasionally, until lightly browned.

3 Remove the bacon using a slotted spoon. Drain on kitchen paper to absorb excess fat. Leave the juices in the pan.

Fish

Master Recipe

Chargrilled Salmon Fillets

Chargrilling on the hob in a ridged, cast-iron pan is a quick, fun way to cook. Food prepared in this way is succulent, full of flavour, and low in fat. For perfect results, accurate timing is essential, so use a timer if you have one. The cooking time given here is for thick fillets; if you can buy only thin ones, cook for about 2 minutes each side.

 Serves 2   **Prep** 10 mins   **Cook** About 6 mins

Ingredients

2 thick pieces of salmon fillet,
125–175g (4½–6oz) each, skin
on, trimmed and pin-boned
2–3 tbsp sunflower oil
salt and freshly ground
black pepper

Special equipment
A ridged cast-iron chargrill pan
for use on the hob

PER SERVING

Calories: 342
Saturated fat: 5g
Unsaturated fat: 19g
Sodium: 61mg

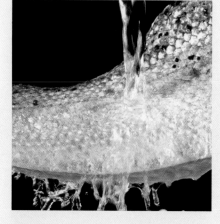

1 Rinse and pat dry the salmon. Preheat the chargrill pan over a high heat for about 10 minutes.

2 Meanwhile, brush both sides of the fillets with oil, then sprinkle them liberally with salt and pepper.

KEY to SUCCESS To test if the pan is hot enough, sprinkle water over it. The water should "dance", then quickly disappear.

3 Reduce the heat to medium. Place the fish, skin-side up, on the pan and grill for 3 minutes, then turn over.

4 Cook the other side. The salmon will be done when it is opaque all along the cut edges.

"Keep the salmon in one place while cooking and the ridges will leave an attractive charred pattern."

Fish Pie with Cheesy Mash Topping

This pie has lots of lovely flavours, so do taste it before seasoning with salt. Since smoked haddock can be a little salty, you may not need as much as usual. If you want to freeze the pie, leave out the eggs. Serve with peas or other green vegetable.

Ingredients

Serves 6

50g (1¾oz) butter, plus extra
   for greasing
4 large eggs
1 onion, peeled and chopped
50g (1¾oz) plain flour
600ml (1 pint) hot milk
1 tbsp chopped fresh dill
juice of ½ lemon
350g (12oz) smoked undyed
   haddock fillet, skinned and cut
   into 2cm (¾in) cubes
350g (12oz) fresh haddock fillet,
   skinned and cut into 2cm (¾in)
   cubes
salt and freshly ground black pepper
100g (3½oz) mature Cheddar
   cheese, grated

FOR THE TOPPING

1kg (2¼lb) floury potatoes, such as
   Maris Piper or King Edward, peeled
   and cut into large chunks
knob of butter
about 6 tbsp hot milk
50g (1¾oz) Parmesan cheese, grated

PER SERVING

Calories: 561
Saturated fat: 14g
Unsaturated fat: 12g
Sodium: 1115mg

Method

1 Preheat the oven to 200°C (fan 180°C/400°F/Gas 6). Grease a 1.7- to 2-litre (3- to 3½-pint) baking dish.

2 Make the topping: place the potatoes in a pan of salted cold water. Bring to the boil and simmer for 15–20 minutes, or until tender. Drain and mash with the butter and milk. Season with salt and pepper. Stir in the Parmesan and set aside.

3 Hard-boil the eggs for 10 minutes, drain, and peel (see p86). Cut each egg into quarters.

4 Make the filling: melt the butter in a large pan, add the onion, and fry for a few minutes. Cover, lower the heat, and simmer for about 10 minutes. Remove the lid, add the flour, stir until combined, and gradually blend in the milk. Stir over a medium heat until thickened and smooth.

5 Add the dill, lemon juice, and haddock. Season with salt and pepper and stir the mixture for a couple of minutes. Remove the pan from the heat, add the Cheddar, stir in the egg quarters, and tip into the baking dish. Spread the cheesy mash over the top.

6 Bake in the oven for 30–40 minutes, or until the pie is bubbling around the edges and piping hot in the centre.

Use hot milk

When making a white sauce or adding milk to mashed potatoes, it's best to use hot milk. Bring the milk to a gentle simmer over a medium heat.

Fry the chopped onion

Heat the butter in a large pan over a medium heat. Add the onions and stir with a wooden spoon to ensure they are coated in butter and will not stick.

Herb-crusted Haddock

This makes a great family supper. Sometimes I make it with salmon fillet instead, or sustainable cod. You can coat the fish in breadcrumbs a few hours in advance then keep it in the fridge until it's time to fry. Serve with green vegetables.

Ingredients

Serves 4

75g (2½oz) fresh white breadcrumbs
6 sprigs of fresh parsley
10 sprigs of fresh dill
grated zest of 1 lemon
2 tbsp plain flour
1 large egg, beaten
4 pieces of fresh unsmoked haddock
   fillet, each weighing 125–175g
   (4½–6oz), skinned
salt and freshly ground black pepper
2 tbsp olive oil
lemon wedges, to serve

PER SERVING

Calories: 348
Saturated fat: 2g
Unsaturated fat: 8g
Sodium: 286mg

Method

1 Make the breadcrumbs in a food processor as shown below, ideally using sliced bread that is a day or two old. If it is too fresh, the bread will stick into a ball rather than form crumbs.

2 Add the parsley and dill sprigs, and the lemon zest, to the breadcrumbs in the food processor and pulse all the ingredients until they make very finely textured crumbs.

3 Lay out 2 plates on the worktop: spread out the flour on one and the breadcrumb mixture on the other. Place a bowl containing the beaten egg between the plates.

4 Prepare each haddock fillet in turn: sprinkle with salt and pepper, then coat with the flour and shake off the excess. Dip each piece in the beaten egg, then coat lightly with the breadcrumb and herb mixture.

5 Heat the oil in a large non-stick sauté pan. Place the fish in the pan and cook over a medium heat for 3 minutes on each side, or until golden brown and crisp. Serve hot, with lemon wedges for squeezing.

DRIED BREADCRUMBS

Dried breadcrumbs are made from bread that has been toasted or baked to remove all the moisture, and they give a crispier texture than fresh crumbs. Make fresh crumbs first, as shown here, then spread them out on a baking tray and bake at 150°C (fan 130°C/300°F/Gas 2) for about 20 minutes, or until golden. Alternatively, dry slices of bread in the oven first, then process into crumbs.

How I make fresh white breadcrumbs

1 For coating food, pure white breadcrumbs look best, so use day-old white bread and cut the crusts off. Three or four slices will make about 75g (2½oz) breadcrumbs.

2 Tear the bread into large pieces and put the chunks into a food processor fitted with the metal blade. Process for a few seconds until the bread makes fine crumbs.

Grilled Trout with Cucumber

I really like the fresh taste of cucumber with the trout in this recipe. Cucumber cooks quickly, so take care not to overcook it – it should still have a little bite. You can grill many other fish, including sea bass and mackerel, the same way.

Ingredients

Serves 4

½ cucumber, peeled
40g (1¼oz) butter
2 tbsp chopped fresh dill
juice of 1 lemon
salt and freshly ground black pepper
4 trout, each weighing 375–425g
  (13–15oz), boned
a few sprigs of dill, to garnish

PER SERVING

Calories: 385
Saturated fat: 7g
Unsaturated fat: 9g
Sodium: 221mg

THE BENEFITS OF TROUT

Trout is an oily fish, which means it is very high in omega 3 and a rich source of other vitamins and nutrients. As well as being very healthy, it is delicious and versatile. In addition to grilling trout you can pan-fry, bake, or roast it, or cook it on the barbecue. It is widely available, either whole or in fillets.

Method

1 Cut the cucumber lengthways in half, scoop out the seeds as shown below, then cut across to make slices no more than 5mm (¼in) thick.

2 Melt half the butter in a pan. Add the cucumber, toss over a low heat for 2 minutes, then remove from the heat and add the chopped dill, lemon juice, and salt and pepper. Stir to mix.

3 Preheat the grill for 5 minutes on its highest setting. Remove the grid of the grill pan and line the grill pan tray with foil.

4 Season the trout inside and out, then spread the remaining butter over the skin. Place the trout in the grill pan tray.

5 Reduce the grill to a medium-high setting and grill the fish, about 10cm (4in) from the heat. After 4–7 minutes, remove the grill pan tray from the heat, carefully turn the trout over, and scatter the cucumber and dill mixture around the fish.

6 Slide the grill pan tray back under the grill and cook the other side of the fish for 4–7 minutes, or until the flesh flakes easily when it is tested with a fork. Serve the fish with the cucumber and garnish with dill sprigs.

Deseed the cucumber

Slice the peeled cucumber in half lengthways, then use a teaspoon to scrape down the inside and scoop out the seeds. Discard the seeds.

Chop the dill

Strip the feathery green leaves from the dill stalks, pile the leaves on a chopping board, and chop them finely. Save a few whole sprigs for garnish.

Seafood Kebabs

These kebabs are great at any time of year, but they're particularly good in summer, cooked on the barbecue. Brush well with marinade and keep an eye on them, as they cook quickly. You'll need eight wooden skewers, allowing for two per person.

Ingredients

Serves 4

500g (1lb 2oz) monkfish fillets, or other firm white fish fillet, such as brill or halibut, skinned
8 raw tiger prawns, peeled and deveined
4 baby courgettes, trimmed and each cut into 4 pieces
16 cherry tomatoes

FOR THE MARINADE

6 tbsp olive oil
1 tbsp balsamic vinegar
3 tbsp chopped fresh tarragon or basil
2 large garlic cloves, peeled and crushed
salt and freshly ground black pepper

PER SERVING

Calories: 341
Saturated fat: 3g
Unsaturated fat: 15g
Sodium: 183mg

USING WOODEN SKEWERS

I prefer wooden skewers to metal ones, which get very hot under the grill. If you're using wooden skewers, soak them in warm water for at least 6 hours before use so they don't burn during cooking.

Method

1 First make the marinade: place all the ingredients in a large non-metallic bowl and stir thoroughly to combine.

2 Remove the central bone from the monkfish if the fishmonger has not done this, as shown below, and cut the fillets into 16 equal-size chunks. Place the fish in the marinade, add the prawns and mix. Cover and refrigerate for up to 6 hours.

3 Line the grill pan with foil. Just before cooking, preheat the grill for 5 minutes on its highest setting.

4 Lift the fish and prawns out of the marinade (reserve the marinade). Thread 2 chunks of fish, 1 prawn, 2 pieces of courgette, and 2 tomatoes onto each of the 8 skewers. Arrange the skewers on the grid of the grill pan and brush with the marinade. Reduce the grill heat to medium-high.

5 Grill the kebabs, about 10cm (4in) from the heat, for about 10 minutes, turning them twice and brushing with the marinade. Check that the fish is opaque in the centre.

6 Serve the fish and vegetables on the skewers on a large platter, or slide them off and serve them on individual plates.

How to fillet and trim a monkfish

1 Lay the monkfish tail on its belly. Using a sharp filleting knife, cut along one side of the backbone with long, sweeping strokes. Turn the fish and repeat on the other side.

2 With the knife at a sharp angle, remove the thin grey-brown membrane that covers the fish, cutting close to the flesh. If left on, this will shrink around the fish, making it tough.

Mary's Secrets of Success

Fish

Seafood Kebabs, pp100–101

1 **When buying fish,** look for firm, moist flesh and ask for it to be cut while you wait. Also, check its aroma. It should have the clean smell of the sea. If it has an unpleasantly "fishy" or ammonia-like odour, it's not fresh.

2 **If buying pre-packaged fish,** check the colour of any liquid that has accumulated in the pack: if it's a white fish the liquid shouldn't be cloudy or off-white.

3 **Try to buy fish that is responsibly sourced.** Look out for the MSC (Marine Conservation Society) ecolabel, which means it has come from a sustainable fishery.

Oven-poached Salmon with Chilli Mayonnaise, pp104–105

4 **If you're unclear about how much fish to allow:** a whole fish weighing 350–500g (12oz–1lb 2oz) is enough for one person; for fillets, allow 125–175g (4½–6oz) per person.

5 **I suggest that you ask** your fishmonger to prepare your fish, especially if you're a new cook. Pin-boning, gutting, filleting, and scaling are all very work-intensive and require expertise.

6 Fish deteriorates quickly: as soon as you get it home, unwrap it, cover with wet kitchen paper, and store in the coldest part of the fridge. Use oily fish the same day; keep white fish no more than 24 hours.

7 Never overcook fish. It's so easy to do and overcooking will really spoil the texture and flavour. Follow the recipes in this book and you can't go wrong.

Chargrilling tuna steaks, p246

8 It's better to buy ready-frozen fish than freeze your own, as it will usually have been frozen while at sea. However, if you have fish to freeze, clean and then wrap it in a double layer of plastic freezer bags.

9 Use frozen white fish within 3 months and oily fish within 2 months. Fish fillets can be cooked from frozen.

10 Fish keeps better in large pieces, so if you're making a dish like fish pie, leave the fish in one piece and cut it as you need it.

Fish Pie with Cheesy Mash Topping, pp94–95

Oven-poached Salmon with Chilli Mayonnaise

Whole salmon makes an impressive centrepiece for a buffet. To serve, cut the flesh off in slices; when it has all been removed from one side, lift off the bone then carefully turn the fish over and slice off portions from the other fillet.

Ingredients

Serves 10–12

olive oil, for brushing
about 3kg (6½lb) whole salmon, cleaned
1 lemon, sliced
4-5 sprigs of fresh dill
salt and freshly ground black pepper
6 tbsp white wine

FOR THE CHILLI MAYONNAISE

300ml (10fl oz) mayonnaise (see p248)
1 tsp finely grated lemon zest
1-2 tbsp lemon juice
3-4 tsp chilli sauce

TO GARNISH

thin slices of cucumber
thin slices of radishes
a few small sprigs of fresh dill
lemon slices
a few sprigs of watercress

PER SERVING

Calories: 765
Saturated fat: 9g
Unsaturated fat: 46g
Sodium: 323mg

TESTING FOR DONENESS

To check if the salmon is cooked, give the middle fin on the back a tug and it should come out easily. Or, insert the tip of a knife in the plumpest part of the flesh, pull the flesh gently back, and check that it no longer looks raw in the middle.

Method

1 Preheat the oven to 150°C (fan 130°C/300°F/Gas 2). Brush a large piece of foil with oil, then lay the salmon on the foil. Place the lemon and dill in the cavity, and season with salt and pepper. Pour the wine over and around the fish, then bring the foil up around it, folding over to seal well.

2 Place the salmon on a large baking tray or shallow roasting tin (you may need to remove the head if the fish will not fit in the tin, otherwise leave it on). Poach the fish in the oven for 1½–1¾ hours.

3 Make the chilli mayonnaise: mix the mayonnaise with the lemon zest and enough lemon juice to taste. Spoon into a serving dish and swirl the chilli sauce through it so it is slightly rippled. Chill until ready to use.

4 When the salmon is cooked, set aside to cool for about 1 hour, still wrapped in its foil parcel. Remove the fins and head, if still on.

5 Carefully slide the salmon onto a large serving platter. Skin and scrape as shown below, then turn the fish over and repeat on the other side.

6 Garnish the top with slices of cucumber and radish, scattered with dill sprigs. Arrange some lemon slices and a few watercress sprigs on the platter around the base of the fish. Serve with the chilli mayonnaise.

Skin and prepare the salmon for serving

1 Use a small sharp knife to peel off the skin from the body, pulling the skin gently with the knife.

2 Gently scrape off the thin brown layer of flesh from the top and sides, leaving behind only the pink flesh.

Sole Fillets with Creamy Pesto Sauce

This is a special occasion fish dish. Your fishmonger may well bone and skin the sole for you, but it's always useful to know how to do it yourself; it's the same technique for all flatfish. Serve the fillets on a bed of buttered leaf spinach.

Ingredients

Serves 4

60g (2oz) plain flour
salt and freshly ground black pepper
2 small lemon sole, each cut
   into 4 fillets and skinned
30g (1oz) butter

FOR THE SAUCE

300ml (10fl oz) double cream
juice of ½ lemon
3 tbsp fresh basil pesto (see p38)
100g (3½oz) sun-blushed tomatoes,
   finely chopped
2 tsp chopped fresh basil, to garnish

PER SERVING

Calories: 735
Saturated fat: 30g
Unsaturated fat: 27g
Sodium: 402mg

Method

1 Sprinkle the flour onto a plate and season with salt and pepper. Dip the 8 fillets into the seasoned flour and shake off any excess.

2 Melt the butter in a large frying pan. When it is foaming, add the fillets and cook for 2 minutes on each side, or until the flesh is opaque and flakes easily. Transfer to warmed serving plates and keep warm.

3 Make the sauce: heat the cream, lemon juice, and pesto in a pan over a medium heat until hot, then add the sun-blushed tomatoes, heat through, and season with salt and pepper. Pour the sauce on top of the sole on the serving plates and scatter with the basil leaves.

Fillet and skin a flatfish the easy way

1 Make a shallow cut all around the edge of the fish and where the head and tail meet the body. Then cut down the centre, through to the bone.

2 Insert the knife between the flesh and bones at the head end. Work along the fish, loosening the flesh to detach the fillet. Repeat on the opposite side.

3 Turn the fish over and remove both fillets in the same way as previously. Check the fillets for stray bones, pulling them out with tweezers.

4 Lay each fillet skin-side down and hold the tail with salted fingers for a firm grip. Holding the knife at an angle, cut the flesh from the skin.

Fishcakes

I do like to fry my fishcakes in butter as I love the flavour. For a less rich result, bake them in the oven on a lined baking sheet. This same mixture can be shaped into smaller cakes and served as a first course with a mayonnaise-based dip.

Ingredients

Makes 4

15g (½oz) butter, plus extra
 for greasing
200g (7oz) smoked undyed haddock
 fillet, skinned
200g (7oz) fresh haddock
 fillet, skinned
salt and freshly ground black pepper
300g (10oz) floury potatoes, such as
 Maris Piper or King Edward, peeled
 and cut into large chunks
2 tbsp chopped fresh parsley
2 tbsp snipped fresh chives
½ tsp finely grated lemon zest
2 tbsp mayonnaise (see p248)
¼ tsp Dijon mustard
2 tsp drained, chopped capers
1 egg, beaten
75g (2½oz) fresh white breadcrumbs
 (see p96)
2 tbsp vegetable oil
lemon wedges, to serve

PER SERVING

Calories: 365
Saturated fat: 4.5g
Unsaturated fat: 13.5g
Sodium: 727mg

Method

1 Preheat the oven to 200°C (fan 180°C/400°F/Gas 6). Grease a large piece of foil with a little butter. Sit both haddock fillets on the foil, season with pepper, then wrap to make a parcel.

2 Place the foil parcels on a baking sheet and bake for 15 minutes until just cooked and opaque. Set aside to cool.

3 Cook the potatoes in boiling salted water until tender, for 10–12 minutes. Drain well, return to the pan, and mash. Tip into a bowl.

4 Stir the parsley, chives, lemon zest, mayonnaise, mustard, and capers into the mashed potato and season with salt and pepper. Break the fish into large pieces and gently stir into the mash without breaking the pieces up too much.

5 Divide the mixture into 4 and shape it into fishcakes as shown below. Dip each fishcake in the beaten egg on both sides so it is well covered, then coat in the breadcrumbs. Pat to reshape. Chill for about 30 minutes.

6 Melt the butter with the oil in a non-stick frying pan. Fry the fishcakes on a medium heat for 4–5 minutes each side. Serve with lemon wedges.

Make crispy, golden fishcakes

1 Shape the mixture into flat cakes, about 2.5cm (1in) thick. You can do this in your hands or on a board. If they stick, dust the surface with flour.

2 Fry the breaded fishcakes until lightly golden. When one side is done, turn them over very carefully with a fish slice and cook the other side.

Poultry and Game

Master Recipe

Roast Chicken with Herb Butter

This is the simplest of roasts yet easily one of the most popular. The herb butter used in cooking the chicken goes into the gravy, making it deliciously rich and full of flavour. You can either serve the bird on a large platter and carve it whole at the table or, if you prefer, carve it in the kitchen and arrange slices on warmed plates.

 Serves 4   **Prep** 25 mins   🕐 **Cook** 1½ hours, plus 5 mins for the gravy

Ingredients

1.5–1.8kg (3lb 3oz–4lb) chicken
1 onion, peeled and cut lengthways
   into sections
1 lemon, cut into 6 wedges

FOR THE HERB BUTTER

85g (3oz) butter (room temperature)
3 tbsp finely chopped fresh parsley
1 tbsp finely snipped chives
   or finely chopped spring onion
1 tsp finely chopped fresh
   tarragon or thyme leaves
1 tsp lemon juice
salt and freshly ground black pepper

FOR THE GRAVY

2 tsp plain flour
300ml (10fl oz) chicken stock
   (see p.126)
4 tbsp white or red wine (optional)

Special equipment
A large roasting tin to hold the chicken
and onion and lemon wedges

PER SERVING

Calories: 662
Saturated fat: 20g
Unsaturated fat: 26g
Sodium: 390mg

Cook's notes

Buy a good chicken
It's well worth buying a good-quality bird; free-range chickens tend to have the best flavour.

Prepare ahead
If you like, you can prepare the chicken and spread it with the herb butter in advance. Keep it covered with foil, in the fridge, for 8–12 hours until you need it. Let it stand at room temperature for about 30 minutes before roasting.

Defrosting frozen chicken
Defrost a frozen chicken thoroughly or it will not cook through. Pierce the wrapping, then stand the bird on kitchen paper in a container. Leave in a cold place overnight (in the fridge it will take 36 hours) until there are no ice crystals remaining in the cavity.

Giblets
If there are giblets inside the chicken, remove them before preparing the bird. You can make a good stock from them (see p138).

Make the herb butter

 Prep 10 mins

1 Put the butter in a bowl and beat it with a wooden spoon to soften it. Add the chopped herbs, spring onion if using, lemon juice, and salt and pepper.

2 Stir the ingredients together, then beat them vigorously until they are evenly combined. Preheat the oven to 200°C (fan 180°C/400°F/Gas 6).

Prepare the chicken for roasting

 Prep 15 mins

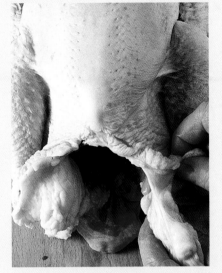

KEY to SUCCESS For the skin to be crisp, it must be completely dry. This is especially important if the bird has been frozen, because it is often quite wet after defrosting.

1 Using your fingers, pull off the excess white fat on either side of the opening at the tail end of the chicken. Discard the unwanted fat.

2 Wipe the inside of the cavity of the chicken with kitchen paper, then use a fresh piece to wipe the skin. This ensures the bird is dry inside and out.

3 Put two or more of the onion wedges inside the main cavity of the chicken before tying up the bird. This will give added flavour.

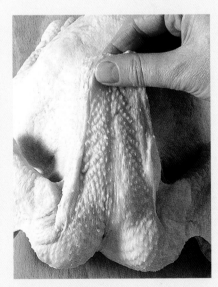

KEY to SUCCESS Tying the chicken with string (trussing) holds the bird together and keeps the stuffing in place.

4 Turn the chicken breast-side down and pull the neck skin over the neck cavity. If you like, cut off the excess skin with scissors to neaten it.

5 Twist the wings round so the tips come up and over the skin to secure it. Turn the chicken breast-side up and tie the legs together with string.

6 Put the chicken breast-side up in the roasting tin and surround it with the remaining onion and lemon wedges. Spread the herb butter liberally all over the bird.

Roast and baste the chicken

 Cook 1¼–1½ hours, plus 15 minutes resting

KEY to SUCCESS If the breast skin shows signs of over-browning during roasting, cover the bird with a "tent" of foil.

1 Put the chicken in the preheated oven for about 20 minutes or until browned, then baste it all over with the buttery cooking juices. Return the chicken to the oven.

2 Roast the chicken for a further 55–70 minutes, or until the juices run completely clear when the flesh is pierced with a sharp knife in the area between the body and leg.

3 When cooked, wrap the bird in a large sheet of foil, then leave it to rest for 15 minutes before you carve (see pp128–29). Remove the onion and lemon from the tin. Make the gravy.

Make the gravy

Cook 5 minutes

KEY to SUCCESS If the gravy is too thick, add more hot liquid. If it is too thin, let it bubble and allow to reduce a little.

1 Tilt the roasting tin so the juices settle in one corner, then spoon off most of the fat (all but about 1½ tablespoons) and discard. Retain the dark juices and scrape the caramelized bits on the base and sides of the tin using a wooden spoon; they will add flavour.

2 Put the tin directly on the hob over a medium heat and sprinkle the flour over the juices in the tin. Using very fast, circular movements, whisk with a coil or balloon whisk for about 2–3 minutes until the flour browns a little and forms a paste.

3 Pour in the hot chicken stock and bring to the boil, whisking all the time. Add the wine, if using, and whisk to mix. Simmer for 2 minutes, then check the seasoning. Pour the finished gravy into a warmed gravy boat or jug and serve immediately.

"Succulent and full of flavour, this roast is a firm family favourite. I serve it with fresh green vegetables, roast potatoes, and bread sauce."

Stir-fried Ginger Chicken

The art of the stir-fry is to cook finely chopped ingredients swiftly in a small amount of hot oil in a wok. For success, you need intense heat under the pan and to keep tossing. Stir-frying is one of the fastest and healthiest methods of cooking.

Ingredients

Serves 4

6 spring onions, trimmed

2.5cm (1in) piece of fresh root ginger, peeled

4 carrots, peeled

1 red pepper, cored and deseeded

1 yellow pepper, cored and deseeded

350g (12oz) skinless, boneless chicken breast

250g (9oz) dried medium Chinese egg noodles

3 tbsp sunflower oil

2 tbsp Chinese rice wine or dry sherry

4 tbsp dark soy sauce

fresh coriander leaves, to garnish

PER SERVING

Calories: 545
Saturated fat: 4g
Unsaturated fat: 15g
Sodium: 1074mg

USING A WOK

A wok should never be more than one-third full, and the food should have room to touch the hot sides of the pan. If you don't have a wok and a shovel, use a large, deep, non-stick sauté pan instead, and toss the ingredients with two wooden spoons. To test the temperature, add a drop of oil; it will sizzle when the wok is ready.

Method

1 Slice the spring onions on the diagonal into short lengths. Cut the ginger into matchsticks. Cut the carrots and peppers into thin sticks no more than 5mm (¼in) thick and 5cm (2in) long. Slice the chicken into thin strips across the grain. Soak and drain the noodles to soften as shown below.

2 Place a wok over a high heat for 1–2 minutes until very hot. Add the oil and heat until it just begins to smoke. Drop the pieces of spring onion and ginger into the hot oil. Stir them around vigorously for about 1 minute, tossing to coat them in the oil.

3 Push the spring onion and ginger to one side. Add the carrots and peppers and stir-fry in the same way for 1–2 minutes, then stir the spring onion and ginger back in.

4 Push the vegetables aside and add the chicken a little at a time. Sizzle the chicken briefly on each side before tossing with the other ingredients for a further 1–2 minutes.

5 Pour in the rice wine or sherry and allow it to bubble briefly. Add the soy sauce and stir to mix with the chicken and vegetables.

6 Add the noodles to the wok and toss to mix. Taste and add more soy sauce if you like. Serve immediately, garnished with coriander.

Soften the noodles

1 Bring plenty of water to the boil in a 5-litre (8¾-pint) pan. Add the noodles and stir to separate them. Remove the pan from the heat.

2 Cover the pan and let stand for 6 minutes. Drain the noodles thoroughly in a colander. Toss the noodles with 1–2 teaspoons of sesame oil, if liked.

Parmesan-crusted Chicken

The cream cheese that coats the chicken creates a moist topping, so there is no need for a sauce with this. In summer, serve it with a green salad and new potatoes; in winter, provide a selection of seasonal green vegetables.

Ingredients

Serves 4

olive oil, for brushing

4 skinless, boneless chicken breasts, about 500g (1lb 2oz) in total

salt and freshly ground black pepper

125g (4½oz) full-fat cream cheese

30g (1oz) sun-blushed tomatoes, chopped

1 garlic clove, peeled and crushed

grated zest of ½ lemon

25g (scant 1oz) fresh white breadcrumbs (see p96)

25g (scant 1oz) Parmesan cheese, grated

2 tbsp snipped chives

1 red pepper, deseeded and cut into 8 wedges

PER SERVING

Calories: 387
Saturated fat: 11g
Unsaturated fat: 12g
Sodium: 284mg

Method

1 Preheat the oven to 200°C (fan 180°C/400°F/Gas 6). Oil the roasting tin or baking tray, as shown below, and lay the chicken in the tin. Brush each chicken breast with a small amount of oil, then season.

2 In a small bowl, mix the cream cheese with the sun-blushed tomatoes, garlic, lemon zest, and black pepper. Set aside.

3 In another bowl, combine the breadcrumbs with the Parmesan and chives, then season well.

4 Spread a quarter of the cream cheese mixture over the top of each chicken breast. Sprinkle the breadcrumb mixture on top of each and pat gently into the cream cheese.

5 Scatter the pepper wedges around the chicken, brush them with oil, and season with black pepper.

6 Bake for about 20 minutes or until the pepper wedges are charred around the edges, the chicken is cooked, and the topping golden.

Oil the roasting tin

Dip a small brush into oil and use it to grease the surface of the roasting tin. Alternatively, use a sheet of kitchen paper dipped in oil.

Cut chunky pepper wedges

Remove the stalk and core from the pepper and cut in half lengthways. Scrape out the white ribs and seeds, then cut each half into quarters.

Thai Green Chicken Curry

Adding flour to a curry isn't traditional, but I find it helps to stabilize the sauce, which can sometimes curdle. If you want extra heat, leave the seeds in the chilli. Stirring the sugarsnap peas in at the last moment retains their colour and texture.

Ingredients

Serves 4

500–550g (1lb 2oz–1¼lb) skinless, boneless chicken breast, sliced into thin strips

2 tbsp Thai green curry paste

2 tbsp vegetable oil

1 large onion, peeled and thinly sliced

2 tsp plain flour

400ml can coconut milk

100–150ml (3½–5fl oz) chicken stock (see p126)

1½ tbsp Thai fish sauce

2 tsp light muscovado sugar

1 green Thai chilli, deseeded and cut into thin strips

salt and freshly ground black pepper

100g (3½oz) sugarsnap peas, halved lengthways

¼ tsp finely grated lime zest

2 tsp lime juice

handful of chopped fresh coriander

PER SERVING

Calories: 428
Saturated fat: 16g
Unsaturated fat: 10g
Sodium: 649mg

Method

1 Marinate the chicken in 1 tablespoon of the curry paste for 30 minutes. Meanwhile, heat the oil in a large frying pan, add the onion, and cook gently over a low heat, stirring occasionally, for about 10 minutes until softened but not browned. Lift out and set aside.

2 Increase the heat to high, put in the chicken and stir-fry for 3 minutes, or until no longer pink. Stir in the other tablespoon of curry paste and the flour, and cook for 1 minute.

3 Reduce the heat and return the onions to the pan. Stir in the coconut milk, 100ml (3½fl oz) of the stock, the fish sauce, sugar, and chilli. Bring to a simmer, cover, and cook gently for about 10 minutes, until the chicken is tender and the sauce is only just boiling. Thin the sauce with the rest of the stock if wished. Taste for seasoning.

4 Meanwhile, blanch the sugarsnap peas in a pan of boiling salted water for 2–3 minutes, or until tender-crisp. Drain.

5 Just before serving, stir the sugarsnaps into the curry to warm through, then add the lime zest and juice and lots of coriander. Serve with white long-grain rice, as shown below.

How I make fluffy white long-grain rice

1 Measure 300ml (10fl oz) rice in a measuring jug, pour it into a sieve and rinse thoroughly until the water runs clear. Drain thoroughly. Put the rice into a large pan with a tight-fitting lid and add 600ml (1 pint) cold water.

2 Add 1 teaspoon salt and bring to the boil. Stir, reduce heat to low, and cover. Simmer gently for 12–15 minutes, until all the water has been absorbed. Take off the heat. Let stand, covered, for 5 minutes. Fluff up grains with a fork.

Mary's Secrets of Success

Poultry and Game

1 **Buy organic, free-range chicken** wherever possible. Choose a fresh-smelling bird with a plump breast and moist, unblemished skin.

Roast Chicken with Herb Butter, pp112–15

2 **Poultry must be kept cool.** As soon as you get the bird home, remove the wrapping and giblets (if there are any), put it on a plate to collect drips, cover it loosely, and store it in the fridge. Always cook poultry by the "use by" date.

3 **To prevent salmonella poisoning,** wash work surfaces, utensils, and hands thoroughly before and after handling raw meat, and don't let the bird or any equipment come into contact with cooked poultry or meat.

4 **Skinning chicken joints** before cooking will reduce fat levels and calories, but the skin does add flavour and make the meat more succulent. A good solution is to cook chicken with the skin on, then pull it off just before serving.

5 **For crispy skin,** make sure the bird is completely dry before roasting.

6 I place fatty birds, such as duck and goose, on a rack, to let the fat drain and keep the skin crisp. Small birds can be cooked upside down until brown, then turned breast-side up for the rest of the cooking time, ensuring they're brown all over.

7 Frozen birds must be thoroughly thawed before cooking. Unwrap, cover loosely with fresh wrapping, and set on a plate in the fridge to thaw. Never refreeze a raw bird.

Traditional Roast Pheasant, pp138-39

8 Always cook poultry thoroughly. To test for doneness, insert a knife into the flesh between the body and leg, or into the thickest part of chicken pieces; the juices should run clear.

Chicken, Leek, and Mushroom Pie, pp126-27

9 Although not essential, sturdy poultry shears make light work of jointing poultry, and a meat thermometer takes the guesswork out of roasting.

10 Whenever I make a Sunday roast I use the carcass for stock (see p126) and any leftover meat for soups, pies, risottos, and salads.

Coq au Vin

You can make this classic dish up to 2 days ahead and just reheat it before serving. It also freezes well after it has been cooked; make sure you defrost thoroughly before reheating. Serve it with mashed potatoes to soak up all the wonderful sauce.

Ingredients

Serves 6

25g (scant 1oz) dried
   porcini mushrooms
1 bottle red wine (750ml/1¼ pints)
15g (½oz) butter
1–2 tbsp olive oil
6 chicken legs
200g (7oz) streaky bacon, sliced
400g (14oz) small shallots, peeled
250g (9oz) chestnut mushrooms,
   halved if large
3 tbsp brandy
45g (1½oz) plain flour
4 sprigs of fresh thyme
2 sprigs of fresh rosemary
2 tbsp tomato purée
2 garlic cloves, peeled and sliced
2 tsp light muscovado sugar
salt and freshly ground black pepper

PER SERVING

Calories: 446
Saturated fat: 6g
Unsaturated fat: 10g
Sodium: 583mg

Method

1 Soak the porcini in 300ml (10fl oz) boiling water for 15 minutes. Pour the wine into a large pan. Add the porcini and their liquid. Boil over a high heat until the liquid has reduced by about a third.

2 Meanwhile, heat the butter and half of the oil in a large, deep frying pan with a lid, or flameproof casserole. Brown the chicken. You may have to do this in batches. Transfer to a plate and set aside.

3 Drain off excess fat from the pan. Tip in the bacon and shallots and fry until starting to turn golden, then remove. Add the chestnut mushrooms, with more oil if needed, and fry for 2–3 minutes. Return the shallots and bacon to the pan. Add the brandy, stirring to deglaze the pan.

4 Put the flour in a jug and slowly stir in a little cold water to make a thin, smooth paste. Add the reduced wine and porcini mixture, stir until smooth, and pour into the pan with the mushrooms, bacon, and shallots. Stir over the heat until the liquid has thickened.

5 Add the herbs, tomato purée, garlic, and sugar. Season with salt and pepper. Return the chicken pieces to the pan and gently push them down into the sauce. Bring to the boil, cover with a lid, and simmer for 1¼–1½ hours, until the chicken is tender. Check the seasoning.

Peel the shallots

Slice off the ends of the shallots with a sharp knife. Carefully peel off the skin with your fingers or using a small, sharp knife. Discard the skin.

Chicken, Leek, and Mushroom Pie

Using ready-cooked chicken means it's quick to make this pie, but you can roast a whole chicken, use the meat for the pie and the bones for stock, saving any leftover stock for soups. The flavour of tarragon is a good partner for chicken.

Ingredients

Serves 4–6

50g (1¾oz) butter
2 large leeks, trimmed and sliced
50g (1¾oz) plain flour, plus
  extra for dusting
300ml (10fl oz) milk
300ml (10fl oz) hot chicken stock
1 tsp Dijon mustard
1 tbsp chopped fresh tarragon
250g (9oz) chestnut mushrooms, sliced
salt and freshly ground black pepper
500g (1lb 2oz) cooked chicken, sliced
50g (1¾oz) Cheddar cheese, grated
500g (1lb 2oz) puff pastry (see p273)
1 egg, beaten

PER SERVING
Calories: 660
Saturated fat: 19g
Unsaturated fat: 20g
Sodium: 560mg

Method

1 Preheat the oven to 200°C (fan 180°C/400°F/Gas 6). Melt the butter in a pan. Add the leeks and fry over a low heat for about 10 minutes. Mix the flour with a little of the milk in a small bowl to make a smooth paste.

2 When the leeks are soft, turn up the heat and add the paste to the pan with the remaining milk and stock. Bring to the boil, stirring all the time, until the sauce is thickened and smooth.

3 Add the mustard and tarragon. Stir in the mushrooms and simmer for 2 minutes. Season with salt and pepper and add the cooked chicken. Remove the pan from the heat and add the cheese. Pour the mixture into a shallow 1.7-litre (3-pint) pie dish and set aside to cool.

4 Meanwhile, make the pastry top. On a lightly floured work surface, roll out the pastry until it is slightly larger than the dish. Cut 4 strips of pastry to the width of the lip of the dish, brush the lip with water, and attach the strips on top. Brush the top of the strips with water, then lay the pastry lid on them and press to seal the edges. Crimp the edges with your fingers.

5 Brush the pastry with egg. Cut any pastry trimmings into leaf shapes, arrange them on top of the pie, then brush with more egg. Using the tip of a sharp knife, create a small steam hole in the centre of the pie. Bake in the oven for about 35 minutes, or until the pastry is crisp and golden.

How I make fresh chicken stock

1 Put a chicken carcass in a large pan. Coarsely chop 1 onion, 2 celery sticks, and 2 carrots, and add to the pan with 1 bay leaf, peppercorns, and herbs.

2 Add cold water to cover, bring to the boil, and skim any scum off the surface. Reduce the heat to a gentle simmer. Cover and cook for 2½–3 hours.

3 Discard the carcass. Strain the liquid through a sieve. Keep leftover stock covered in the fridge for up to 3 days, or in the freezer for up to 6 months.

Masterclass

Roasting and Carving Poultry

Poultry is the term for all birds reared for their meat, the most familiar being chicken, turkey, duck, and goose. All are great roasted whole. To get the most from your bird, and for good presentation, it's well worth learning how to carve properly.

Chicken and turkey

Roasting chicken is shown on pp112–15, and for roasting turkey see the chart opposite. Use the same carving technique for both, although for a large bird you may need to bone the thigh and slice it and the drumstick meat into strips.

How to carve a chicken

1 After the bird has rested for 15 minutes, place it breast-side up on a board. Hold it steady with a carving fork and cut between the leg and breast.

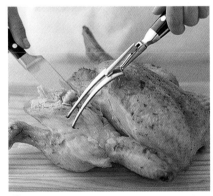

2 Using both the knife and the fork, lift the leg backwards to ease the bone away from the body. Repeat the process for the other leg.

3 Slice downwards along one side of the breastbone to free the breast, keeping the knife close to the bone. Repeat on the other side of the bone.

4 Slice the two breast halves in half, then carve them into equal-sized slices with the knife held on the diagonal. Remove the wings.

5 Slice each leg through the joint to separate the thigh and drumstick. Place the white and dark meat on a warmed platter and serve.

Bread sauce

This creamy sauce is delicious with roast turkey and chicken.

Insert 8 whole **cloves** into 1 **onion**. Put in a pan with 900ml (1½ pints) **milk**, 1 **bay leaf**, and 6 **peppercorns**. Bring to the boil, remove from the heat, cover, and leave to infuse for 1 hour. Strain the milk and return to the pan. Add 175g (6oz) **fresh white breadcrumbs**, bring to the boil, stirring. Simmer for 2–3 minutes. Season with **salt** and **pepper**, and stir in 60g (2oz) **butter**. Serve hot.

Duck and goose

Both duck and goose are fatty, so to reduce fattiness prick the skin before roasting and place on a rack over a roasting tin. Duck and goose have denser flesh than chicken and turkey so they are "jointed" rather than sliced into strips.

How to carve a duck or goose

1 Place the duck or goose on a board, breast-side up. First, cut away the legs by slicing through the joints with a carving knife.

2 Slice downwards along one side of the breast-bone to free the breast meat. Repeat on the other side of the bone.

3 Cut each piece of breast on the diagonal into thick slices. Serve each person some breast meat and either a wing or a leg.

Stuffing a bird

Stuff the neck end only, not the body cavity (this should be stuffed only with herbs and other flavourings). Place the bird tail-end down in a bowl. Pull back the neck skin and spoon in the stuffing. Pull the skin over the stuffing and secure with a skewer.

ROASTING POULTRY: TEMPERATURES AND TIMINGS

Use these timings as a guide, but bear in mind sizes of birds and oven temperatures vary, and you must always check poultry is well cooked, preferably using a meat thermometer. I recommend roasting large birds in a high oven first, to get heat quickly into the bird, then reduce the temperature and continue cooking more gently until done. If the bird is browning too quickly, cover it with foil.

BIRD	SIZE	OVEN TEMPERATURE	TIMING	INDICATOR OF DONENESS
CHICKEN	1.5-2.25kg (3lb 3oz–5lb)	Preheat oven to 200°C (fan 180°C/400°F/Gas 6)	20 mins per 450g (1lb), plus 20 mins Rest 15 mins	Juices must be clear (needs to be cooked through); meat thermometer reading 75°C (170°F)
TURKEY	6-7kg (12–14lb) (medium-sized turkey)	Preheat oven to 220°C (fan 200°C/425°F/Gas 7), then reduce temperature to 160°C (fan 140°C/325°F/Gas 3)	40 mins, then roast further for 3–3½ hours Rest 30-45 mins	As for chicken
DUCK	1.8-2.5kg (4–5½lb)	Preheat oven to 220°C (fan 200°C/425°F/Gas 7), then reduce temperature to 160°C (fan 140°C/325°F/Gas 3)	1 hour, then roast further for 30 mins Rest 15 mins	As for chicken
GOOSE	5-6kg (10–12lb)	Preheat oven to 220°C (fan 200°C/425°F/Gas 7), then reduce temperature to 180°C (fan 160°C/350°F/Gas 4)	30 mins, then roast further for 1½–2 hours Rest 15 mins	As for chicken

Tandoori Chicken

This Indian classic is ideal served with rice or warm naan bread. For a fresh-tasting accompaniment, make a raw relish of finely chopped red onion, chopped coriander, and diced, skinned tomato, well seasoned with a dash of olive oil and lemon juice.

Ingredients

Serves 4

4 skinless, boneless chicken breasts
lemon slices, to garnish

FOR THE MARINADE

100ml (3½fl oz) plain full-fat yogurt
3 tbsp sunflower oil
1 small onion, peeled and grated
1 garlic clove, peeled and crushed
2 tsp ground ginger
1 tsp ground turmeric
1 tsp Madras (hot) curry powder

PER SERVING

Calories: 195
Saturated fat: 2g
Unsaturated fat: 6g
Sodium: 110mg

TANDOORI DISHES

The term "tandoori" is used to describe a dish cooked in a tandoor – a vat-shaped clay oven, traditionally heated with charcoal or wood. The heat that builds up inside is fierce, so the chicken cooks extremely quickly, sealing the juices of the bird and keeping it moist. At home, when cooking without a tandoor, it is important to preheat the grill to its maximum setting. Marinating the chicken before cooking ensures it is tender and full of flavour.

Method

1 Mix all the ingredients for the marinade together in a large, non-metallic bowl with 2 tablespoons cold water.

2 Trim the chicken breasts and make slits in the flesh as shown below. Add the chicken to the bowl and coat in the marinade.

3 Cover the bowl with cling film and leave to marinate in the fridge for 8–24 hours, so the chicken has time to absorb all the flavours.

4 Line a grill pan with foil and preheat the grill on its highest setting for about 5 minutes before cooking.

5 Drain the chicken breasts, shaking off excess marinade, and discard the marinade. Arrange the chicken on the grid of the grill pan. Reduce the grill heat to a medium-high setting.

6 Grill the chicken, about 10cm (4in) from the heat, for about 6 minutes on each side. Test the chicken is ready by inserting a knife into the thickest part of the breast. The chicken is done when the juices run clear.

7 You can either slice the chicken before serving or leave the breast whole. Garnish with lemon slices.

Prepare the chicken breasts

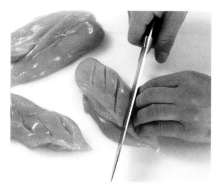

1 Strip the white tendon away from the underside of the breast using a paring knife. The tendon is sinewy and chewy; discard it.

2 To keep skinless breasts succulent and tender during cooking, score the top on the diagonal with a chef's knife before marinating them.

Duck Breasts with Redcurrant Sauce

I remove the skin before cooking duck breasts, as it's hard to get the skin really crisp without overcooking the meat. If you like the skin, cook it separately and slowly in a frying pan or low oven, and when crisp, snip it with scissors into strips.

Ingredients

Serves 4

4 duck breasts, about 200g (7oz) each, skin removed
salt and freshly ground black pepper
about 2 tbsp olive oil

FOR THE SAUCE

2 shallots, peeled and finely chopped
1 garlic clove, peeled and finely chopped
1 sprig of fresh thyme
250ml (9fl oz) red wine
1 tsp demerara sugar
5 tbsp redcurrant jelly
10g (¼oz) butter, cut into small pieces

PER SERVING

Calories: 439
Saturated fat: 6g
Unsaturated fat: 15g
Sodium: 242mg

Method

1 Season the duck breasts with salt and pepper, then brush them all over with 1 tablespoon of olive oil.

2 Heat a non-stick frying pan or sauté pan until hot. With the heat on medium-high, lay the oiled duck breasts in the pan, skinned-side down, and fry for 5–6 minutes (depending on how plump they are) without disturbing them. If browning too quickly, reduce the heat to medium.

3 When browned, turn and fry for a further 5–6 minutes. Remove the duck from the pan, transfer to a dish, cover with foil, and keep warm.

4 Make the sauce: heat the remaining tablespoon of oil in the same pan the duck was cooked in and put in the shallots, garlic, and thyme, stirring to scrape up any sticky bits from the bottom of the pan. Fry for about 2 minutes, or until the shallots are soft and starting to brown.

5 Pour in the wine, add the sugar, and bring to the boil, then simmer to reduce by one-third. Stir in the redcurrant jelly, let it melt, then simmer for a few minutes until the sauce looks rich and slightly syrupy.

6 Remove the pan from the heat, discard the thyme, and whisk in the butter, piece by piece. Taste for seasoning. Serve each duck breast with a spoonful or two of the sauce spooned over.

Chop the shallots finely

Slice horizontally towards the root, leaving the slices attached at the root end, then slice through vertically. Finally, cut across to make fine dice.

66 However busy we are, we always like to sit down together for meals. The kitchen table is the perfect place to catch up with the family. 99

Game Casserole

You can buy packets of mixed boneless game from some supermarkets or butchers; alternatively, make up your own mix, including pheasant and venison. This dish goes particularly well with mashed potatoes and savoy cabbage.

Ingredients

Serves 6

3 rashers dry-cure smoked
  bacon, diced
45g (1½oz) butter
900g (2lb) boneless mixed game,
  trimmed and cut into 4cm (1½in)
  cubes
2 red onions, peeled and chopped
25g (scant 1oz) flour
300ml (½ pint) red wine
300ml (½ pint) game stock or chicken
  stock (p126)
2 tbsp redcurrant jelly
dash of gravy browning (optional)
salt and freshly ground black pepper
1 bouquet garni
chopped fresh parsley, to garnish

PER SERVING

Calories: 357
Saturated fat: 5.5g
Unsaturated fat: 6.5g
Sodium: 370mg

GRAVY BROWNING

Made from caramel, molasses, and spices, liquid gravy browning gives casseroles a lovely appetizing rich brown colour. It can be a little hard to track down, but it's well worth having a bottle in your storecupboard. It is not to be confused with gravy powder or granules.

Method

1 Place a large, deep non-stick frying pan with a lid or flameproof casserole over a medium heat. When the pan is hot, add the bacon and fry until crisp. Remove the bacon with a slotted spoon, transfer it to a plate, and set aside.

2 Melt the butter in the pan, add the game and onions, and fry for about 2 minutes, stirring all the time with a wooden spoon.

3 Add the flour, as shown below, then blend in the red wine, stock, redcurrant jelly, and gravy browning, if using. Stir well to combine.

4 Bring to the boil, season with salt and pepper, and add the bouquet garni. Reduce the heat to low and cover the pan with a lid.

5 Gently cook for about 2½–3 hours. Halfway through cooking, increase the heat and bring to the boil again for 2 minutes, then reduce the heat again and return to simmering.

6 Check that the meat is tender and the sauce thick. Serve garnished with chopped parsley.

Make a fresh bouquet garni

Hold together 2–3 sprigs of thyme, 1 bay leaf, and 5–6 parsley stalks. Wind a piece of string around the herbs and tie securely.

Thicken the sauce

Sprinkle the flour over the meat, then stir to mix. Cook over a medium heat for 2–3 minutes, stirring occasionally, until the flour is browned.

Traditional Roast Pheasant

Available from mid-autumn to late winter, pheasants are traditionally sold as a brace (in pairs), but they're also available individually. Serve with redcurrant jelly, bread sauce, sautéed potatoes, and minted peas and courgettes (see pp212–13).

Ingredients

Serves 4

2 pheasants, giblets (if any) reserved
85g (3oz) butter (room temperature)
salt and freshly ground black pepper
4 streaky bacon rashers
a few sprigs of watercress, to garnish

FOR THE GRAVY

1 tsp plain flour
300ml (10fl oz) pheasant giblet stock
   (see box, below) or chicken stock
   (see p126)
1 tsp redcurrant jelly
dash of gravy browning (optional)

PER SERVING

Calories: 581
Saturated fat: 19g
Unsaturated fat: 22g
Sodium: 625mg

GIBLET STOCK

You might find giblets inside the birds, and if so it's well worth making stock from them. Fry them in a little oil in a large pan until lightly browned. Stir in 1 litre (1¾ pints) water and bring to the boil. Skim any scum off the surface. Add 2 quartered onions, 1 chopped celery stick, 1 chopped carrot, 1 bouquet garni, and a few black peppercorns. Simmer for about 1 hour. Strain, then cool.

Method

1 Preheat the oven to 200°C (fan 180°C/400°F/Gas 6). Spread the pheasants with the butter and season. Lay two bacon rashers crossways over each breast.

2 Place the pheasants in a roasting tin and cook in the oven for 1 hour, or until tender, basting once.

3 Test the pheasants by inserting a fine skewer in the thickest part of a thigh; the juices should run clear when they are cooked.

4 Lift the pheasants onto a warmed serving platter, cover with foil, and keep warm while you make the gravy.

5 Pour off all but 1–2 tablespoons of the fat from the roasting tin, reserving any juices and sediments. Place the tin on the hob over a medium heat, heat until sizzling, then add the flour, stock, redcurrant jelly, and gravy browning, if using, as shown below. Taste for seasoning. Strain into a warmed jug or gravy boat.

6 Garnish the roasted pheasants with the watercress sprigs, then carve and serve with the hot gravy.

How I make a rich, meaty gravy

1 Add the flour to the juices in the roasting tin. Whisk briskly, stirring in the caramelized bits from the base and sides. Cook for 2–3 minutes, until you have a well-browned paste.

2 Gradually add the stock, redcurrant jelly, and gravy browning, if using, whisking constantly. Bring to the boil, whisk until smooth and thickened, then simmer for another 2–3 minutes.

Meat

Master Recipe

Steak with Onion Marmalade

Onion marmalade makes a lively accompaniment to steaks and is also extremely versatile. It's a good idea to make twice the amount, as it will keep in the fridge (see below). I find it particularly useful to have on hand for stirring into gravies and sauces, or you can even use a spoonful or two to line the base of a bacon quiche.

 Serves 4 **Prep** 5 mins  **Cook** 1¼ hours

Ingredients

4 ribeye or fillet steaks, about
   115–175g (4–6oz) each, trimmed
1 tbsp olive oil

FOR THE ONION MARMALADE

3 large onions, about 750g
   (1lb 10oz) in total
2 tbsp olive oil
1 tbsp light muscovado sugar
salt and freshly ground
   black pepper
2 tsp balsamic vinegar

Special equipment
A large frying pan with a lid for making the marmalade and a ridged cast-iron chargrill pan for the steaks; alternatively, use a large non-stick sauté pan for the steaks

PER SERVING
Calories: 409
Saturated fat: 7g
Unsaturated fat: 17g
Sodium: 89mg

Cook's notes

Steak cuts
Ribeye and fillet steaks are both recommended here, as they are the most tender cuts. If you use sirloin, beat the steaks out between two sheets of cling film, pounding them with a wooden rolling pin.

Prepare ahead
You can cook the onion marmalade up to 1 week ahead and reheat it on the hob when making the steaks.

Make the onion marmalade

 **Prep** 5 mins  **Cook** 1 hour 10 mins

1 Using a chef's knife, cut the onion lengthways in half. Peel off the skin, leaving the root on to keep the onion halves together. Lay each half cut-side down on the board and slice across (not lengthways).

KEY to SUCCESS You want the heat high enough for the onions to start cooking but not so high they turn brown.

Master Recipe

2 Heat the oil in a large frying pan over a high heat until hot. Add the onions and fry for a few minutes, stirring and ensuring they are all coated with oil.

3 Add the sugar and seasoning and stir to mix. Cover the frying pan with a lid and simmer over a low heat for about 1 hour, or until the onions are very soft.

4 Turn up the heat to get rid of excess moisture, add the vinegar, and check the seasoning. Keep the sauce warm while you grill or fry the steaks.

Cook the steaks

🕐 **Cook** 4–6 mins

KEY to SUCCESS Never salt steaks before grilling or pan-frying, as it draws out the juices.

1 Preheat the chargrill pan or sauté pan over a high heat until piping hot. While the pan is heating, season the steaks with pepper and brush one side with oil.

2 Add the steaks, oil-side down, and grill or fry for about 2 minutes on each side for medium rare. You may need to cook in batches; if so, keep the cooked steaks warm.

3 Just before serving, sprinkle the steaks with salt and more pepper if you like, and top each with a large spoonful of the warm onion marmalade.

"I like my steak medium rare, or pink; if you prefer yours well done, just add another minute or two to the cooking time."

Classic Beef Casserole

The great advantage of a casserole is that it can be made well ahead and the flavour will develop and improve with time. This recipe is for a rich, hearty stew, so it's the perfect choice for winter, served with creamy mash and seasonal green vegetables.

Ingredients

Serves 6

2 tbsp sunflower oil
900g (2lb) braising steak, trimmed
   and cut into 2cm (¾in) cubes
2 leeks, trimmed and sliced
2 carrots, peeled and diced
4 level tbsp plain flour
150ml (5fl oz) port or strong red wine
600ml (1 pint) beef stock
1 tbsp redcurrant jelly
1 tbsp Worcestershire sauce
2 bay leaves
salt and freshly ground black pepper
225g (8oz) chestnut mushrooms
a few sprigs of parsley, to garnish

PER SERVING

Calories: 345
Saturated fat: 4g
Unsaturated fat: 9g
Sodium: 244mg

Method

1 Preheat the oven to 160°C (fan 140°C/325°F/Gas 3). Meanwhile, heat the oil in a large flameproof casserole and, over a medium heat, quickly brown the beef all over. Remove the meat with a slotted spoon and set aside. You may need to do this in batches.

2 Add the leeks and carrots to the casserole and brown over a high heat. Add the flour and stir to coat the vegetables.

3 Blend in the port or wine and the stock. Add the redcurrant jelly, Worcestershire sauce, bay leaves, and salt and pepper. Cut the mushrooms into quarters and add them to the casserole with the beef.

4 Bring to the boil, cover with a lid, and cook in the oven for 2–2½ hours, or until the beef is tender. Before serving, remove the bay leaves and garnish each plate with sprigs of parsley.

VARIATION Venison and Beef Casserole Replace half of the beef with stewing venison, cut into the same-sized cubes.

How I make a rich beef stock

1 Put 2kg (4½lb) beef bones into a large roasting tin. Add 2–3 chopped onions, celery stalks, and carrots (or carrot tops). Roast at 230°C (fan 210°C/450°F/Gas 8) for 30 minutes.

2 Transfer the bones and vegetables to a large, deep pan with fresh rosemary, thyme, parsley, and peppercorns. Pour over enough cold water to cover. Bring to the boil and skim off the scum.

3 Cover and simmer gently for 4–6 hours. Discard the bones and strain into a large heatproof jug or bowl. Keeps for up to 3 days in the fridge and 6 months in the freezer.

Perfect Burgers

Simple is often best – which is what these burgers are. If you like, add a little horseradish sauce or Dijon mustard to give extra kick. Grilling burgers is a healthy option, but if you prefer you can fry them in a non-stick frying pan.

Ingredients

Serves 6

1kg (2¼lb) minced beef
2 small onions, peeled and grated
2 tbsp chopped fresh parsley
salt and freshly ground black pepper
dash of Tabasco sauce
2–4 tbsp sunflower oil
6 burger buns, to serve

PER SERVING

Calories: 454
Saturated fat: 10g
Unsaturated fat: 18g
Sodium: 166mg

FILLINGS AND RELISHES

Sliced pickled gherkins, crispy lettuce, rocket, and sliced white or red onion all make great, crunchy accompaniments to burgers. They are also delicious served with tomato relish and mayonnaise, particularly if it's home-made (see p248); you can add Dijon mustard to shop-bought mayonnaise if you wish.

Method

1 Place the minced meat in a bowl with the onion. Add parsley, salt and pepper, and the Tabasco and mix together lightly with your hands until everything is thoroughly combined.

2 Form the mixture into 6 large burgers as shown below, using wet hands to prevent the mixture sticking. Ideally, chill the burgers for at least 30 minutes before grilling. This will allow the meat to firm and helps it to stay together when cooking.

3 Line the grill pan with foil and preheat the grill for about 5 minutes before cooking. Brush the burgers with oil on one side. Lay them, oiled-side down, on the grill and brush the tops with oil.

4 Grill, about 10cm (4in) from the heat, for about 2–3 minutes on each side for rare burgers, 4–5 minutes for medium, and 6 minutes for well done. Serve in a burger bun with side salad and additional fillings and relishes if you wish (see box, left).

VARIATION Lamb Burgers Use lean, minced lamb instead of beef. Replace the parsley with the same amount of fresh chopped mint and add 1 tablespoon redcurrant jelly instead of the Tabasco.

Shape the burgers

With wet hands, divide the mixture into even-sized pieces and roll each out into a ball. Flatten the balls slightly to form a burger shape.

Beef Wellington

A luxurious main course for high days and holidays. I've used middle-cut beef fillet, as it is one even-sized piece, so it cooks evenly all the way down. Instead of buying pâté, you could make your own chicken liver and aubergine pâté (see pp56–57).

Ingredients

Serves 4–6

1kg (2¼lb) piece of middle-cut beef fillet, trimmed
freshly ground black pepper
2 tbsp sunflower oil
25g (scant 1oz) butter (room temperature)
flour, for dusting
350g (12oz) puff pastry (see p273)
250g (9oz) smooth chicken liver or pork pâté (optional)
1 large egg, beaten

PER SERVING

Calories: 681
Saturated fat: 17g
Unsaturated fat: 24g
Sodium: 416mg

Method

1 Preheat the oven to 220°C (fan 200°C/425°F/Gas 7). Season the beef with pepper, brush it with oil, and brown and roast as shown below.

2 Roll out the pastry on a lightly floured surface to a rectangle 3 times wider than the beef and about 20cm (8in) longer.

3 Place the cooled beef in the middle of the pastry. Spread the top of the fillet with pâté, if using, and bring the two long sides up over the beef to meet in the middle with a 2.5cm (1in) overlap. Brush the underside of the overlap with beaten egg and press to seal. Place the parcel seam-side down on a baking sheet, trim the ends of the pastry, leaving enough to fold underneath, and tuck the edges under.

4 Brush the pastry case with beaten egg, as shown below. Roll the pastry trimmings into a long strip. Cut into thin strips and arrange in a criss-cross pattern on top of the parcel. The beef can be baked at this stage, or wrapped in cling film and kept in the fridge for up to 12 hours.

5 Preheat the oven to the same temperature as before. Brush the pastry case with beaten egg again and bake for 30 minutes. If the pastry browns too quickly, cover with foil. Leave the beef to rest for 10–15 minutes, then cut it into thick slices to serve.

How I prepare the beef and pastry case

1 Heat a large non-stick frying pan over a high heat until hot and brown the seasoned beef fillet very quickly to seal the juices. Make sure you brown all the sides.

2 Transfer the browned fillet to a small roasting tin, spread with the butter, and roast for 18–20 minutes if you like it medium rare, or slightly longer for well done. Leave the fillet to cool.

3 Encase the beef spread with pâté in the pastry, as described in steps 2 and 3, above. Using a pastry brush, lightly spread a thin layer of beaten egg over the pastry case, to glaze.

Masterclass

Roasting and Carving Beef

I like to serve roast beef the traditional way, with Yorkshire puddings (see pp228–29), roast potatoes (see pp172–73), red-wine gravy, and horseradish sauce. Allow 225–350g (8–12oz) of meat per person for joints on the bone and 100–175g (3½–6oz) for boneless ones. You can serve beef rare to well done, as you prefer.

Roasting know-how

Always bring meat to room temperature before roasting, and preheat the oven to the correct temperature. One of the best joints is sirloin on the bone, shown below. First, trim off all but a thin layer of fat and season with salt and pepper.

How to roast and carve beef on the bone (sirloin)

  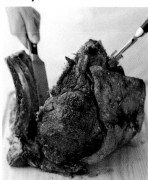 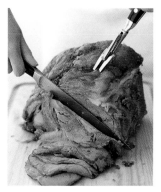

1 Place the joint in a roasting tin with the ribs facing upwards. Brush with olive oil. If you have a meat thermometer, insert it in a thick part of the meat.

2 Roast the beef (see opposite), basting with fat halfway through. Transfer the beef to a carving board, cover with foil, and leave to rest before carving.

3 To carve, first free the meat from the bone. Holding the beef steady with a fork, cut between the meat and bones using a sawing action with a sharp knife.

4 Once the meat is free from the bone, turn the joint so that the fat is uppermost. Cut thin vertical slices with the knife, again using a sawing action.

Creamed horseradish sauce

This smooth sauce is a perfect partner for beef, and is also good mixed into mash.

Mix 2-3 tbsp grated **fresh horseradish** with 1 tbsp **white wine vinegar** in a bowl. In another bowl, whisk 150ml (5fl oz) **double cream** or **whipping cream** until thick. Fold the cream into the horseradish mixture, and add **salt**, **pepper**, and **caster sugar** to taste. Cover the sauce and leave to chill until ready to serve with the beef.

Pot-roasting

Some beef cuts, such as silverside and brisket, are too lean to be roasted in the oven and are better pot-roasted. This involves browning the meat in a flameproof casserole on the hob, then adding liquid (usually wine) and vegetables and simmering, covered, for several hours. A pot-roast is a great one-pot dish and the meat will be beautifully tender.

ROASTING BEEF: BEST CUTS, TEMPERATURES, AND TIMINGS

The timings for roast beef will depend on the weight of the joint and how you like it cooked. Beef on the bone will take a little longer to cook than boneless joints, and benefits from a very hot oven at the start. Cover meat with foil if it's browning too quickly.

CUT	DESCRIPTION	OVEN TEMPERATURE	TIMING	INDICATOR OF DONENESS
SIRLOIN	Best roasting joint for beef on the bone (see opposite). Tender and marbled with fat. Also available without the bone, when it cooks a little quicker	**On the bone** Preheat oven to 220°C (fan 200°C/425°F/Gas 7), then reduce heat to 180°C (fan 160°C/350°F/Gas 4)	15 mins, then roast further as follows: **Rare:** 20 mins per 450g (1lb), plus 20 mins **Medium:** 25 mins per 450g (1lb), plus 20 mins **Well done:** 30 mins per 450g (1lb), plus 20 mins Rest 20 mins	**Rare:** juices will be pink; meat thermometer reading 50°-65°C (120-150°F) **Medium:** juices will be clear; meat thermometer reading 70°C (160°F) **Well done:** juices will be clear; meat thermometer reading 75-80°C (165-175°F)
		Boneless joint Preheat oven to 190°C (fan 170°C/375°F/Gas 5)	25 mins, then roast further as follows: **Rare:** 20 mins per 450g (1lb), plus 20 mins **Medium:** 25 mins per 450g (1lb), plus 25 mins **Well done:** 30 mins per 450g (1lb), plus 30 mins Rest 20 mins	
RUMP	Boneless joint with a coarser grain and less fat than sirloin	As for sirloin (boneless joint)	As for sirloin (boneless joint)	As for sirloin
TOPSIDE/TOP RUMP	Boneless, less expensive, and leaner than sirloin	As for sirloin (boneless joint)	As for sirloin (boneless joint)	As for sirloin
RIBEYE	Good marbled joint, either with a bone or boneless	As for sirloin (on the bone or boneless joint)	As for sirloin (on the bone or boneless joint)	As for sirloin
RIB OF BEEF	From the shoulder end of the sirloin, this is a less expensive, but excellent bone-in joint	As for sirloin (on the bone)	As for sirloin (on the bone)	As for sirloin
FILLET/ TENDERLOIN	Expensive, very tender, lean, and boneless. Often roasted whole or divided into large pieces	**Middle-cut fillet** Preheat oven to 220°C (fan 200°C/425°F/Gas 7)	Brown meat in hot oil in a sauté pan to seal all over, then place in a roasting tin and roast for 10-12 mins per 450g (1lb) for medium rare Rest 10-15 mins	Juices will be slightly pink; meat thermometer reading 65-70°C (150-160°F)

Herby Meatballs with Tomato Sauce

These meatballs make a delicious supper for the whole family. If you want to spice the dish up a bit, add a splash of Tabasco to the sauce as well as to the meatball mixture. Serve with spaghetti and extra Parmesan grated over the top.

Ingredients

Serves 4–6

450g (1lb) minced beef

75g (2½oz) fresh white breadcrumbs (see p96)

75g (2½oz) Parmesan cheese, grated, plus extra to serve

2 tbsp chopped fresh parsley

1 tbsp chopped fresh thyme

1 egg, beaten

a few drops of Tabasco

salt and freshly ground black pepper

2 tbsp sunflower oil

FOR THE SAUCE

1 tbsp olive oil

1 onion, peeled and finely chopped

1 garlic clove, peeled and crushed

2 x 400g cans chopped tomatoes

2 tbsp tomato purée

1 tsp light muscovado sugar

PER SERVING

Calories: 545
Saturated fat: 13g
Unsaturated fat: 21g
Sodium: 493mg

Method

1 Place the beef, breadcrumbs, cheese, parsley, thyme, egg, and Tabasco into a large bowl. Add salt and pepper to taste. Mix well with your hands until everything is thoroughly combined.

2 Shape the mixture into 24 even-sized meatballs as shown below, or by rolling them on a floured work surface.

3 Heat the sunflower oil in a large non-stick frying pan. Add the meatballs and brown over a high heat until golden all over. You may need to do this in batches. Remove and drain on kitchen paper.

4 Make the tomato sauce: heat the olive oil in a large non-stick frying pan with a lid or a flameproof casserole over a high heat. Add the onion and garlic and fry gently for a few minutes. Reduce the heat, cover with a lid, and simmer for about 15 minutes, or until the onions are soft.

5 Remove the lid, add the tomatoes, tomato purée, and sugar, and season with salt and pepper. Bring to the boil.

6 Return the browned meatballs to the pan, cover again, and simmer gently for about 20 minutes, or until the meatballs are cooked through.

Shape and fry the meatballs

1 Using dampened hands, take small amounts of the beef mixture and roll into 5cm (2in) meatballs.

2 Fry the meatballs gently in oil for about 5 minutes, carefully turning them over as they brown.

Chilli Con Carne

Unlike most chilli recipes, which use minced beef, this is made with braising steak and combines fresh chillies and chilli powder for a unique taste. After cooling the dish, it can be kept in the fridge for up to 3 days. It tastes even better made ahead.

Ingredients

Serves 4

2 tbsp sunflower oil
700g (1lb 9oz) braising steak, trimmed
    and cut into 2cm (¾in) cubes
2 onions, peeled and finely chopped
1 garlic clove, peeled and crushed
1–2 fresh chillies, deseeded and
    finely chopped
25g (scant 1oz) plain flour
2–3 tsp chilli powder, to taste
400g can chopped tomatoes
2 tbsp tomato purée
1 beef stock cube
salt and freshly ground black pepper
2 x 400g cans red kidney beans,
    drained and rinsed
1 large red pepper, cored,
    deseeded, and diced
Tabasco sauce (optional)

PER SERVING

Calories: 577
Saturated fat: 14g
Unsaturated fat: 7g
Sodium: 628mg

Method

1 Preheat the oven to 150°C (fan 130°C/300°F/Gas 2). Pour 1 tablespoon of the oil into a large flameproof casserole and, over a medium heat, brown the beef all over. Using a slotted spoon, transfer the cubes to a plate. You may need to do this in several batches.

2 Add the remaining oil to the casserole, heat over a medium heat for 1 minute, then add the onions, garlic, and chillies. Cook for 3 minutes, stirring to loosen the residue from the bottom.

3 Add the flour and chilli powder and stir for 3–4 minutes. Add the tomatoes and meat with its juices, then the tomato purée. Dissolve the stock cube in 425ml (14½fl oz) boiling water and add to the casserole.

4 Stir until just bubbling, season, cover, and transfer to the oven. Cook for 1½ hours, then add the beans and diced pepper. Re-cover and return to the oven for a further 30 minutes.

5 Before serving, test a piece of the meat by biting into it to make sure it is tender. Taste the sauce to check the seasoning and add a few drops of Tabasco if you think it needs more heat.

Deseed and chop fresh chillies safely

1 Wearing rubber gloves to protect your hands, cut the chilli lengthways in half with a paring knife. Scrape out the seeds and membrane with the tip of the knife and discard.

2 Flatten the chilli with your hand and slice lengthways into thin strips, then gather the strips together and cut across into very fine dice. Do not touch your eyes or the chilli will burn.

Mary's Secrets of Success

Meat

1 **Make sure the cut** and the cooking method are compatible – lean meat is ideal for quick cooking, such as pan-frying, stir-frying, or grilling; tougher cuts need longer, slower cooking.

Hoisin Pork Stir-fry, pp160-61

2 **As a rule of thumb,** when calculating how much meat to serve I allow 100–175g (3½–6oz) of boneless meat per person, and 225–350g (8–12oz) if the meat has quite a bit of bone.

3 **Trim off excess fat** before cooking and remove any visible gristle, sinew, and tough connective tissue. However, do retain a thin layer of fat, as it keeps meat moist during cooking and improves flavour.

Steak with Onion Marmalade, pp142-45

4 **If grilling or frying steaks,** chops, or bacon rashers, slash or snip any fat at intervals to prevent the meat curling up during cooking.

5 **Marinate very lean joints** to be roasted or lean cuts to be grilled or barbecued to keep them succulent.

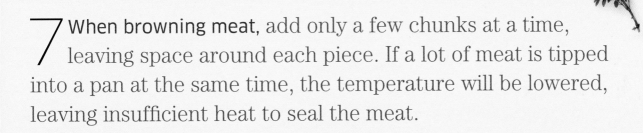

6 Beat out rump steaks, pork fillet, and thin cuts to tenderize them. Place the meat between two sheets of cling film and pound with a wooden rolling pin.

7 When browning meat, add only a few chunks at a time, leaving space around each piece. If a lot of meat is tipped into a pan at the same time, the temperature will be lowered, leaving insufficient heat to seal the meat.

8 I prefer to make slow-cooked meat dishes, such as casseroles, several days ahead rather than on the day of eating – the cooling and reheating process really improves the flavour.

Classic Beef Casserole, pp146–47

9 Store all meat in the fridge, with raw kept separate from cooked and on a lower shelf in order to prevent contaminating any food below.

10 Freeze only very fresh meat, wrapping it tightly first. Mince and sausages can be stored for up to 3 months; offal, chops, and cutlets for up to 4 months; joints and steaks for up to 6 months.

Hoisin Pork Stir-fry

The advantage of a stir-fry is that you can prepare all the ingredients ahead, then it's really quick to cook when you want to eat. If you don't have a wok and are using a frying pan instead, you may have to cook the food in two batches.

Ingredients

Serves 4

2 carrots, peeled
200g (7oz) baby sweetcorn
4-6 spring onions, trimmed
100g (3½oz) fresh beansprouts
8 thin slices of lemon
400g (14oz) pork fillet (tenderloin)
3 tbsp sunflower oil
1 garlic clove, peeled and crushed
5 tbsp hoisin sauce
2 tbsp Chinese rice wine or dry sherry
fresh coriander leaves, to garnish

PER SERVING

Calories: 348g
Saturated fat: 4g
Unsaturated fat: 15g
Sodium: 1168mg

Method

1 Cut the carrots into thin sticks, as shown below, and the sweetcorn into 4cm (1½in) lengths. Slice the spring onions on the diagonal. Prepare the beansprouts as shown below. Cut the lemon slices into quarters.

2 Beat out the pork fillet by placing it between two sheets of cling film and pounding it with a wooden rolling pin or the bottom of a heavy saucepan. Slice the fillet into thin strips as shown below.

3 Heat a wok over a high heat for 1–2 minutes until very hot. Add 2 tablespoons of the oil and heat until it just begins to smoke. Add the carrots, sweetcorn, spring onions, and lemon and stir-fry over a medium heat for 2 minutes, or until the sweetcorn is tender.

4 Remove the vegetables with a slotted spoon. Add half the pork and stir-fry for 3 minutes. Remove with the slotted spoon. Heat the remaining tablespoon of oil in the wok, add the rest of the pork and the garlic and stir-fry for 3 minutes.

5 Return the vegetables and pork to the wok, add the hoisin sauce and rice wine or sherry and stir-fry until bubbling. Add the beansprouts and toss to mix. Serve immediately, garnished with coriander leaves.

Cut the carrots into sticks

Cut the carrots lengthways into thin slices, about 5mm (¼in) thick. Stack the carrot pieces and slice again lengthways into parallel strips, or sticks, no more than 5mm (¼in) wide.

Prepare the beansprouts

Pick over the beansprouts, discarding any that are discoloured. Remove the fine roots and any green hulls. Rinse the sprouts in cold running water in a colander and drain well.

Slice the pork fillet

Trim off any fat from the pork fillet. Using a chef's knife held diagonally, cut the fillet into very thin slices. The thinner you cut the slices, the quicker the pork will cook.

Sausage, Mustard Mash, and Onion Gravy

This is true comfort food and certainly a great favourite with nearly everyone – vegetarians apart! It was served at a winter wedding I attended a few years ago, and it proved to be more popular than a classic buffet.

Ingredients

Serves 4

1 tbsp olive oil
8 good-quality large sausages
salt and freshly ground black pepper

FOR THE MASH

800g (1¾lb) floury potatoes, such as
   King Edward or Maris Piper, cut into
   large chunks
30g (1oz) butter
1 heaped tbsp Dijon mustard
about 4 tbsp hot milk

FOR THE GRAVY

2 onions, peeled and thinly sliced
1 tbsp plain flour
400ml (14fl oz) hot vegetable stock
   (see p30)
2 tsp redcurrant jelly
dash of Worcestershire sauce

PER SERVING

Calories: 528
Saturated fat: 12.5g
Unsaturated fat: 19g
Sodium: 1137mg

FRYING SAUSAGES

Some people prick sausages before cooking to ensure they don't burst. However, if you fry the sausages over a low heat this will not be necessary. Also, they will cook and colour evenly over a low heat.

Method

1 Heat the oil in a large frying pan, add the sausages, and fry over a low heat for about 20 minutes, turning occasionally until golden brown all over. Remove the sausages and set aside. Leave about 2 tablespoons of oil and juices in the pan; discard any excess.

2 Meanwhile, cook the potatoes as shown below. Drain in a colander then return to the pan and mash (see p166). Add the butter and mustard, and enough milk to give a creamy consistency. Season and keep warm.

3 Make the gravy: return the frying pan to a medium heat, stir the onions into the juices in the pan and cook, stirring occasionally, for about 10 minutes or until the onions are very soft and turning a rich golden brown.

4 Stir in the flour and cook for 1 minute. Slowly stir in the stock, scraping up sticky bits from the base of the pan as you go. Bring just to a boil, then lower the heat and simmer for 2–3 minutes. Stir in the redcurrant jelly and season to taste, adding a dash of Worcestershire sauce.

5 Place the sausages in the onion gravy and warm through over a low heat. Serve with the mash.

Boil the potatoes for mash

Put the potato chunks in a large pan filled with enough cold water to cover. Bring to the boil, add salt, and simmer for 15–20 minutes until tender.

Slice the onions

Cut the onion in half lengthways, using a chef's knife. Peel off the skin, leaving the root on. Lay one half cut-side down and slice across. Discard the root end.

Masterclass

Roasting and Carving Pork

One of the great advantages of roast pork over other meats is the crispy crackling. You can make it either by cooking the pork in a very hot oven for part of the time, or by removing the skin and cooking it separately on a rack in a roasting tin in the top of the oven. My favourite accompaniments are apple sauce and savoy cabbage.

Roasting know-how

Always bring pork to room temperature before roasting. Most cuts suitable for roasting are available boned and rolled, and can be stuffed. Pork shoulder is usually slow-roasted, as shown below, to make it extra tender and flavoursome.

How to roast and carve a boneless pork shoulder

1 For crispy crackling, score the skin of the pork in close, parallel lines using a very sharp knife. You can ask your butcher to do this if you prefer.

2 Massage the surface of the skin generously with coarse sea salt and freshly ground black pepper, then rub a little olive oil into the skin.

3 Put the pork, skin-side up, in a roasting tin with onions, lemons, and herbs. Roast (see opposite) without basting. Check it is cooked through.

4 Holding the meat firm with a carving fork, slice between the crackling (cooked skin) and the meat so the crackling lifts off in one piece.

5 Use a pair of kitchen scissors or a sharp knife to cut through the crackling, to give shorter slices that are easier to serve and eat.

6 To carve, steady the joint by piercing it with a carving fork. Cut neat, thick vertical slices with a carving knife using a sawing action.

Fresh apple sauce

The traditional accompaniment for roast pork, apple sauce is very easy to make.

Peel, core, and slice 500g (1lb 2oz) **cooking apples** and put into a pan with the finely grated zest of 1 **lemon** and 2–3 tbsp water. Cover tightly and cook gently for about 10 minutes until soft. Stir in 30g (1oz) **caster sugar**. Beat the sauce until smooth, then stir in 15g (½oz) **butter** if you like. Serve warm or cold, as you prefer. Apple sauce keeps up to 3 days in the fridge, covered.

Stuffing pork

Loin of pork and other boned cuts can be rolled around a savoury stuffing, which adds moisture and flavour to the meat during cooking and makes it easier to carve. Open out the meat and spread it with the stuffing, leaving a small border clear around the edge, roll it up, and tie string around the meat at regular intervals to hold it in shape. Remove the string before carving.

ROASTING PORK: BEST CUTS, TEMPERATURES, AND TIMINGS

Roast pork (except belly and gammon) in a very high oven to begin with, to produce crispy crackling, then roast at a lower temperature until cooked through. Cover the meat with foil if it's browning too quickly. Timings are for boneless joints and depend on their weight.

CUT	DESCRIPTION	OVEN TEMPERATURE	TIMING	INDICATOR OF DONENESS
SHOULDER	On the bone or boneless (see opposite); usually slow-roasted	Preheat oven to 220°C (fan 200°C/425°F/Gas 7), then reduce heat to 180°C (fan 160°C/350°F/Gas 4)	30 mins, then roast for a further 25 mins per 450g (1lb), plus 20 mins. Rest 20–30 mins	Juices must be clear (needs to be cooked through); meat thermometer reading 80–90°C (175–195°F)
LEG	Prime roasting joint, either roasted with the bone in or boned and rolled	As for shoulder	As for shoulder	As for shoulder
LOIN	Tender loin joints on the bone with skin on, or boned and skinless	As for shoulder	As for shoulder	As for shoulder
BELLY	An inexpensive, fatty cut, boned and rolled as a joint; best slow-roasted	Preheat oven to 150°C (fan 130°C/300°F/Gas 2), then increase oven temperature to 220°C (fan 200°C/425°F/Gas 7)	3–4 hours, then roast further for 30–35 mins to brown. Rest 20–30 mins	As for shoulder
GAMMON	A cured joint from the hind legs; gammon is sold raw and needs to be cooked (ham is cooked or dry-cured); serve hot or cold	Preheat oven to 220°C (fan 200°C/425°F/Gas 7)	Boil on the hob for 30 mins per 450g (1lb), then remove the skin, score the fat, and add the flavourings; roast to glaze for 20–25 mins. Rest 20–30 mins	As for shoulder

Cottage Pie

This is a real family classic. If I don't have a bottle of red wine open, I tend to use an inexpensive port that I usually have in my cupboard, as being a fortified wine it keeps well. I like to serve it with a green vegetable, such as broccoli, for colour.

Ingredients

Serves 6

1 tbsp vegetable oil
1 large onion, peeled and chopped
750g (1lb 10oz) minced beef
2 carrots, peeled and diced
1 celery stick, trimmed and diced
115g (4oz) chestnut
    mushrooms, chopped
150ml (5fl oz) red wine
30g (1oz) plain flour
300ml (10fl oz) beef stock
    (see p146)
1 tbsp redcurrant jelly
1 tbsp Worcestershire sauce
2 tsp fresh thyme

FOR THE TOPPING

900g (2lb) floury potatoes, such as
    Maris Piper or King Edward, peeled
    and cut into large chunks
30g (1oz) butter, plus an extra knob
    for the surface
about 4 tbsp hot milk
salt and freshly ground black pepper

PER SERVING

Calories: 540
Saturated fat: 13g
Unsaturated fat: 15g
Sodium: 250mg

Method

1 Heat the oil in a large sauté pan. Add the onion and fry until starting to brown. Put in the mince and brown as shown below, then add the carrots, celery, and mushrooms and fry for 1 minute. Pour in the wine and let it bubble for 2–3 minutes over a high heat until reduced by about two-thirds. Sprinkle in the flour and cook, stirring, for about 1 minute.

2 Pour in the stock and stir until thickened. Mix in the redcurrant jelly, Worcestershire sauce, and thyme. Bring to a simmer and cook, covered with a lid, for 45 minutes to 1 hour.

3 Meanwhile, make the topping: cook the potatoes in a large pan of boiling salted water for 15–20 minutes until tender. Drain well in a colander, then return to the pan and mash as shown below. Preheat the oven to 200°C (fan 180°C/400°F/Gas 6).

4 Taste the meat mixture for seasoning and adjust if necessary. Spoon it into a large baking dish.

5 When the meat has cooled slightly, spread the mashed potato on top, making swirling patterns over the surface with a fork. Dot the top with the extra knob of butter, then bake for about 20–25 minutes, or until the potato is golden and the meat bubbling.

Brown the mince

Heat the oil in a pan and when hot add the mince, breaking it up with a wooden spoon. Fry, stirring frequently, until the meat is no longer pink.

Make creamy mash

Using a potato masher, mash the potatoes with butter and hot milk. For extra-creamy mash, finish with a hand whisk. Season with salt and pepper.

Lamb Shanks with Red Wine Sauce

This is a great dish to serve as an informal lunch when you want something that can be made ahead. It also freezes well. It's cooked in the oven for a long time and slowly, until the lamb is wonderfully tender. Lovely with mashed potatoes.

Ingredients

Serves 6

2 tbsp olive oil

6 small lamb shanks (about 275g/9½oz each)

2 onions, peeled and thinly sliced

1 large carrot, peeled and sliced into rounds

2 garlic cloves, peeled and crushed

1 tbsp finely chopped fresh rosemary

50g (1¾oz) plain flour

300ml (10fl oz) red wine

300ml (10fl oz) chicken stock (see p126)

1 tbsp tomato purée

1 tbsp Worcestershire sauce

1 tbsp light muscovado sugar

PER SERVING

Calories: 446
Saturated fat: 7.5g
Unsaturated fat: 12.5g
Sodium: 243mg

Method

1 Preheat the oven to 160°C (fan 140°C/325°F/Gas 3). Heat 1 tablespoon of the oil in a large frying pan with a lid or flameproof casserole over a high heat. Brown the lamb shanks in 2 batches until golden. Remove with a slotted spoon, transfer to a plate, and set aside.

2 Heat the remaining oil in the pan, add the onions and carrot and fry until the onions are starting to soften. Add the garlic and rosemary and fry for about 30 seconds, stirring constantly.

3 Mix the flour in a small bowl with a little of the red wine to make a smooth paste. Add the paste to the pan with the remaining wine and stock, and stir until the sauce has thickened.

4 Add the tomato purée, Worcestershire sauce, and sugar. The sauce should be quite thick at this stage. Return the lamb shanks to the pan and bring the sauce to the boil.

5 Cover the pan with a lid. If you are using a casserole, transfer it to the oven for 2½–3 hours, checking after 2 hours, until the lamb is completely tender and almost falling off the bone. Alternatively, if you are using a deep frying pan, continue the final simmering on the hob over a low heat for about 3 hours, stirring occasionally.

Cut the carrots into rounds

Slice the carrots crossways into rounds with a chef's knife. For quick and even cooking, make the rounds about 5mm (¼in) thick.

Chop the rosemary

Remove the leaves from their woody stalks and gather in a pile. Hold the tip of the blade against the board and rock the blade back and forth to chop.

Roasting and Carving Lamb

Roast lamb is a Sunday lunch favourite, particularly in spring, when the meat is melt-in-the-mouth tender and at its peak of flavour. I serve it with minted peas and courgettes (see pp212–13), roast potatoes (see pp172–73), gravy, and mint sauce.

Roasting know-how

Remove the meat from the fridge at least 30 minutes before roasting; if chilled, it will take longer to cook and will steam rather than roast. Leaving the meat to rest after roasting allows the juices to settle, making the meat easier to carve.

How to roast and carve a leg of lamb

1 Using a sharp knife, make deep slits over the fat side of the joint using the tip of a small, sharp knife. Insert rosemary sprigs and garlic cloves, sliced in half lengthways, into the incisions.

2 Brush the fat with olive oil and season liberally with salt and black pepper. Place the joint in a large roasting tin and put into a preheated oven (see opposite).

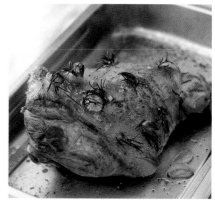

3 Roast the lamb, basting with the juices halfway through. When the meat is cooked to your liking, transfer the joint to a board, cover with foil, and let rest in a warm place before carving.

4 To carve, place the joint meat-side up and slice off the front of the thigh by following along the bone with your knife. Turn the meat over and do the same on the other side.

5 Cut the remaining lamb from the bone. Lay the chunks of boneless meat on their flat, cut sides and carve thick vertical slices. Lay the slices on a warmed platter to serve.

Fresh mint sauce

A traditional accompaniment to roast lamb, mint sauce tastes so much better if it's home-made.

Strip the leaves off a bunch of **fresh mint** and finely chop the leaves using a chef's knife or mezzaluna (half-moon chopper). You should have about 3 tbsp chopped mint. Put in a pan with 1–2 tbsp **caster sugar**, to taste, and pour over 2–3 tbsp boiling water. Stir for 2–3 minutes. Add 1–2 tbsp **white wine vinegar**, to taste. Let stand for about 1 hour before serving.

Stuffing lamb

If you ask the butcher to remove the leg or shoulder bone, you can fill the lamb with stuffing. This adds flavour and moisture and makes carving a lot easier. There are two ways to stuff a joint. You can keep the lamb whole and stuff the cavity (as shown here). Alternatively, cut it open to lie flat, spread it with stuffing, then roll up the joint, tying string around to secure (as shown on p165).

ROASTING LAMB: BEST CUTS, TEMPERATURES, AND TIMINGS

Give leg, saddle, and shoulder of lamb a quick blast in a high oven until brown on top, then reduce the heat and roast until tender. If the meat is browning too quickly, cover it with foil. Timings depend on the weight and are for slightly pink lamb.

CUT	DESCRIPTION	OVEN TEMPERATURE	TIMING	INDICATOR OF DONENESS
LEG	Prime roasting cut on the bone (see opposite) or boned and rolled	Preheat oven to 220°C (fan 200°C/425°F/Gas 7), then reduce temperature to 180°C (fan 160°C/350°F/Gas 4)	20 mins, then roast for a further 20 mins per 450g (1lb), plus 20 mins Rest 15–30 mins	Juices will be slightly pink; meat thermometer reading 75°C (170°F)
SADDLE	Most expensive roasting joint with the bone in or boned and rolled	As for leg joint	As for leg joint	As for leg joint
LOIN FILLETS/ CANON OF LAMB	Lean, tender fillets; expensive and very quick to cook	Preheat oven to 220°C (fan 200°C/425°F/Gas 7)	Brown meat in hot oil in a sauté pan, then roast for 8–10 mins Rest 5–10 mins	As for leg joint
SHOULDER	May be the whole shoulder, or halved into blade end or knuckle end; bone-in or boned and rolled; sometimes quite fatty	As for leg joint	As for leg joint	As for leg joint
BEST END OF NECK	When trimmed and the chine bone is removed, best end becomes a rack (see pp176–77). Two racks leaning together form a guard of honour; two formed into a circle and stuffed make a crown roast	**Rack of lamb** Preheat oven to 220°C (fan 200°C/425°F/Gas 7) (see also p176)	Brown meat in hot oil in a sauté pan, skin-side down, then roast for 25–30 minutes Rest 10 mins	As for leg joint

Lamb Chops with Fresh Mint and Redcurrant Sauce

These chops make a great supper dish and go perfectly with crispy roast potatoes (see below). You can get the potatoes roasting, then just before you're ready to eat, pan-fry the chops and make the mint and redcurrant sauce.

Ingredients

Serves 4

4 lamb loin chops, trimmed
salt and freshly ground black pepper
100ml (3½fl oz) red wine
2 tbsp chopped fresh mint
1 tbsp redcurrant jelly

PER SERVING

Calories: 256
Saturated fat: 5g
Unsaturated fat: 7g
Sodium: 107mg

Method

1 Heat an empty non-stick sauté pan over a high heat for 2 minutes, or until piping hot. Season both sides of each chop with pepper, then place the chops in the hot pan.

2 Reduce the heat to medium and set a timer for 3–4 minutes, depending on the thickness of the chops and how you like your lamb cooked. When the time is up, turn the chops over and reset the timer for 3–4 more minutes. Lift out the chops, transfer to a dish, and keep warm.

3 Pour the red wine into the pan and boil until reduced to 5 or 6 tablespoons. Add the mint and redcurrant jelly, and stir until the jelly has melted. Taste for seasoning. Put the chops on 4 serving plates, pour over the sauce and serve with the roast potatoes and a green vegetable.

How I make crispy roast potatoes

1 Preheat the oven to 220°C (fan 200°C/425°F/Gas 7). Place 1kg (2¼lb) floury potatoes, peeled and cut, in a pan of cold water. Bring to the boil, add salt, simmer for 5 minutes. Drain. Return to the pan and shake to fluff up the edges.

2 Put 3 tablespoons of goose fat in a roasting tin and place in the oven for about 5 minutes until very hot. Lift out the tin, add the potatoes, and turn to coat them in the hot fat. Return the tin to the oven for 5–10 minutes.

3 Shake the tin gently (this stops the potatoes sticking), then roast for 45 minutes, turning occasionally. When the potatoes are crisp, golden brown, and cooked through, lift them out with a slotted spoon.

“ *I shop locally whenever I can. I stock up on staples and buy fresh vegetables, fruit, meat, fish, and bread as and when I need them.* **”**

Herb-crusted Rack of Lamb

This special occasion roast is delicious served with roast potatoes (see p172) or potatoes dauphinoise (see pp208–209) and a green vegetable. By cooking it on the rack, the lamb is kept very moist and succulent.

Ingredients

Serves 6

2 racks of lamb
1 large egg, beaten
45g (1½oz) fresh white breadcrumbs (see p96)
2 tbsp finely chopped fresh parsley
2 tbsp finely chopped fresh mint
2 spring onions, finely chopped
1 garlic clove, peeled and crushed
grated zest of 1 lemon
salt and freshly ground black pepper

PER SERVING
Calories: 385
Saturated fat: 11g
Unsaturated fat: 11g
Sodium: 197mg

ABOUT RACK OF LAMB
Also known as best end of neck, rack of lamb is a tender joint for roasting or grilling. A single rack, which is one side of the upper ribcage, usually comprises 6-9 cutlets. Butchers generally sell it with the backbone and skin removed and the rib bones cleaned of meat.

Method

1 Preheat the oven to 200°C (fan 180°C/400°F/Gas 6). Trim excess fat off each rack of lamb if necessary, as shown below, and brush beaten egg over the fat that remains.

2 Combine the breadcrumbs, herbs, spring onions, garlic, and lemon zest in a bowl. Add salt and pepper and 1 tablespoon of the remaining beaten egg and mix together to form a wet paste. Divide the paste in half, and spread one portion over the fat side of each rack.

3 Place the rack, herb-crust up, in a roasting tin, with the bones pointing towards the centre.

4 Roast the lamb for 20 minutes for rare meat, 35 minutes for medium, and 40 minutes for well done.

5 Remove from the oven, cover with foil, and leave to rest in a warm place for 10 minutes before slicing into individual cutlets.

Trim the rack of lamb

Using a sharp chef's knife, trim away most of the fat from the meat. Do not remove it all, as it will keep the lamb succulent and add flavour.

Chop the mint

Place the mint on a chopping board and rock the mezzaluna backwards and forwards. If you don't have a mezzaluna, use a chef's knife.

Lamb Tagine

This is great for making ahead, as the flavours have time to mellow. You don't need a special tagine dish – a large flameproof casserole dish is fine. I've used shoulder, which is well marbled with fat and has good flavour, but you can also use neck fillet.

Ingredients

Serves 6

2 tbsp sunflower oil

2 large onions, peeled and
   finely chopped

2 garlic cloves, crushed

750g–1kg (1lb 10oz–2¼lb) boneless
   shoulder of lamb, trimmed and cut
   into 4cm (1½in) cubes

25g (scant 1oz) plain flour

2 tsp ground paprika

2 tsp ground cumin

2 tsp ground cinnamon

2 tsp ground turmeric

salt and freshly ground black pepper

400ml (14fl oz) tomato passata

250g (9oz) ready-to-eat dried
   apricots, halved

2 tbsp chopped fresh flat-leaf parsley,
   to garnish

PER SERVING

Calories: 452
Saturated fat: 11g
Unsaturated fat: 16g
Sodium: 237mg

Method

1 Preheat the oven to 160°C (fan 140°C/325°F/Gas 3). Heat the oil in a large pan or flameproof casserole. Add the onions and garlic and fry over a medium heat for 10 minutes, or until golden, stirring occasionally.

2 Add the cubes of lamb to the pan, then sprinkle in the flour together with the paprika, cumin, cinnamon, turmeric, salt, and pepper. Cook, stirring and turning the lamb, for 5 minutes.

3 Pour the passata into a measuring jug and make up to 600ml (1 pint) with cold water. Pour onto the lamb, stirring. Add the apricots.

4 Heat until a few bubbles appear, then cover the pan and cook in the oven for about 2½ hours, or until tender.

5 Serve the tagine with freshly made couscous, as shown below, and garnish with chopped flat-leaf parsley.

How I make light, fluffy couscous

1 Bring 600ml (1 pint) water to the boil in a 2.5-litre (4¼-pint) pan. Add 1½ teaspoons salt, 1½ tablespoons olive oil, and 375g (13oz) couscous to the boiling water.

2 Remove the pan from the heat, stir, and cover with a lid. Let stand for 5 minutes, return to the hob, and cook over a medium heat, stirring with a fork, for 3–5 minutes.

Pasta and Rice

Master Recipe

Spaghetti Bolognese

Named after the city of Bologna in northern Italy, Bolognese is a rich, meaty sauce, or *ragù*, based on beef and soffritto – a finely chopped mixture of celery, onion, carrot, and garlic. Here I've served it with spaghetti, but in Italy it would be more traditional to use a chunkier pasta, such as tagliatelle, penne, or rigatoni.

Serves 6   **Prep** 10 mins   **Cook** 1¼–1½ hours

Ingredients

1 small celery stick, trimmed
1 onion, peeled
1 carrot, peeled
2 large garlic cloves, peeled
2 tbsp olive oil
25g (scant 1oz) butter
500g (1lb 2oz) minced beef
1 tbsp plain flour
3 tbsp tomato purée
150ml (5fl oz) beef stock
    (see p146)
150ml (5fl oz) red wine
400g (14oz) can chopped tomatoes
nutmeg
salt and freshly ground
    black pepper
500g (1lb 2oz) spaghetti
grated Parmesan cheese, to serve

Special equipment
A deep, heavy pan or casserole for the sauce and a 5-litre (8¾-pint) pan for the pasta. Spaghetti tongs are useful but not essential.

PER SERVING
Calories: 567
Saturated fat: 10g
Unsaturated fat: 16g
Sodium: 173mg

Cook's notes

Shopping tips
Fresh Parmesan cheese is fairly expensive, but infinitely superior to the cheaper pre-grated varieties. Buy it in chunks and either grate it with a box grater (fine or coarse, as you wish), or shave off curls with a vegetable peeler as and when needed.

Prepare ahead
You can keep the sauce in the fridge, covered, for up to 3 days, or in the freezer for up to 3 months.

Prepare the vegetables

Prep 10 mins

Pull off and discard any tough strings from the back of the celery stick. Using a chef's knife, finely chop the celery, onion, and carrot. Crush the garlic in a garlic press.

Fry the vegetables and meat

 **Cook** 10 mins

1 Pour the oil into the deep, heavy pan, then add the butter. Place the pan over a medium heat and leave it until the butter melts and foams. Turn the heat down to low.

KEY to SUCCESS Cook the soffritto slowly, as this will release the full flavour of the vegetables.

2 Add the vegetables to the oil and butter and cook over a low heat, stirring constantly, for about 5 minutes or until softened but not browned.

3 Add the meat to the softened vegetables, break it up with a wooden spoon, then cook until it loses its redness, stirring frequently. Sprinkle over the flour and stir in well.

Master Recipe

183

Cook the sauce

🕐 **Cook** 1¼ hours

KEY to SUCCESS Make sure steam can still escape from the pan by not covering it fully.

1 Add the tomato purée, beef stock, red wine, and tomatoes. Using a nutmeg grater held over the pan, add about 8 gratings of fresh nutmeg. Add salt and pepper.

2 Bring the sauce to the boil, stirring constantly, then reduce the heat to very low so that the mixture is just simmering. Partially cover the pan.

KEY to SUCCESS If there is any surplus fat on the top of the sauce at the end, blot it off with kitchen paper.

KEY to SUCCESS Don't skimp on the cooking time. This is the secret of a good Bolognese.

3 Cook the sauce for about 1 hour, stirring every 15 minutes or so to check that the mixture is not sticking to the bottom of the pan. If it is, add a little water and stir well.

4 The sauce will be thick and glossy. Taste for seasoning. Keep the sauce warm and cook the pasta according to the instructions. Pour the sauce over the pasta and mix.

"A rich Bolognese is the basis of many wonderful Italian dishes, so it's well worth mastering."

Pasta Primavera

Primavera means springtime, so when asparagus is in season I often make this for a spring lunch. To make it at other times, just vary the green vegetables – perhaps use broccoli instead of asparagus. If using fresh pasta, cook it for about 3 minutes.

Ingredients

Serves 4–6

1 red pepper, halved and deseeded

1 large onion, peeled and roughly chopped

225g (8oz) asparagus, trimmed and cut into 2.5cm (1in) lengths

100g (3½oz) sugarsnap peas, sliced in half lengthways

300g (10oz) dried penne

100ml (3½fl oz) double cream

60g (2oz) Parmesan cheese, coarsely grated

salt and freshly ground black pepper

juice of ½ lemon

25g (scant 1oz) toasted pine nuts

1 tbsp torn fresh basil leaves

PER SERVING

Calories: 538
Saturated fat: 12g
Unsaturated fat: 12g
Sodium: 131mg

Method

1 First, chargrill the pepper: place the halves under a hot grill, 10cm (4in) from the heat, for 10 minutes until charred. Seal in a plastic bag and leave to cool. Peel and discard the skin. Slice the flesh into large pieces.

2 Plunge the onion into a pan of salted boiling water for 10 minutes. After 9 minutes add the asparagus, boil for another minute, then add the sugarsnaps and boil for 2 minutes. Drain, rinse in cold water, and shake well.

3 Cook the penne as shown below, then return it to the pan with the vegetables. Add the red pepper, cream, and cheese, season and mix. Squeeze over the lemon, scatter over the pine nuts and basil, and serve.

Cook the pasta to perfection

1 Bring about 3 litres (5¼ pints) water to the boil in a 5-litre (8¾-pint) pan. Add 3 teaspoons salt, then the pasta, and bring back to the boil.

2 Cook, uncovered, over a high heat for the recommended time (about 10–15 minutes). Stir with a spoon, to prevent the penne sticking together.

3 Just before the time is up, lift out some pasta and pinch it with your fingers, or taste it. It should be tender, but retain some bite (*al dente*).

4 Remove the pan from the heat and drain the pasta in a large colander. Shake the colander vigorously to drain off as much water as possible.

Tagliatelle with Tomato Sauce

It's best to use tinned tomatoes for cooking if you can't get really ripe, juicy fresh ones, but if you have a glut use a couple of pounds of fresh ones instead. Skin and chop them first and include the seeds. For extra colour, add some tomato purée.

Ingredients

Serves 6

2 tbsp olive oil

1 large onion, peeled and finely chopped

2 x 400g cans chopped tomatoes

2 tsp caster sugar

1 tsp chopped fresh thyme

1 bay leaf

salt and freshly ground black pepper

500g (1lb 2oz) dried tagliatelle

small fresh basil leaves, to garnish

grated Parmesan cheese, to serve

PER SERVING

Calories: 373
Saturated fat: 1g
Unsaturated fat: 5g
Sodium: 56mg

Method

1 Heat the oil in a medium pan until hot. Add the onion and cook over a low heat until softened but not brown, stirring occasionally.

2 Add the tomatoes, sugar, thyme, bay leaf, and salt and pepper to the pan. Stir well. Bring to the boil over a high heat, then reduce the heat to low and simmer gently, uncovered, for about 30 minutes or until thickened, stirring occasionally.

3 Remove the bay leaf and check the seasoning. Keep hot over a low heat while cooking the tagliatelle. Drain the tagliatelle in a colander, then put it in a warmed large bowl. Pour over the tomato sauce and toss to mix. Serve immediately, sprinkled with the basil leaves and cheese.

The best way to chop an onion

1 Using a chef's knife, cut the onion lengthways in half. Peel off the skin, leaving the root on.

2 Hold one half cut-side down. Make 2 or 3 horizontal cuts through it, cutting up to, but not through, the root end.

3 Cut the onion vertically now, slicing down through the layers, again cutting up to, but not through, the root end.

4 Cut the onion across the vertical slices to get even dice. Discard the root end. Repeat for the other half.

Meat Lasagne

The key to a good lasagne is to get the correct balance of pasta to sauce. I find two layers of lasagne sheets for this amount of Bolognese and white sauce ideal. For variety, you might like to try green lasagne sheets, which contain spinach.

Ingredients

Serves 4

butter, for greasing
1 quantity Bolognese sauce (see pp182–85)
50g (1¾oz) Parmesan cheese, grated
about 6 sheets no pre-cooking required dried lasagne

FOR THE WHITE SAUCE
(Makes 600ml/1 pint)

40g (1¼oz) butter
40g (1¼oz) plain flour
600ml (1 pint) hot milk
salt and freshly ground black pepper
a few gratings of nutmeg

PER SERVING

Calories: 772
Saturated fat: 22g
Unsaturated fat: 21g
Sodium: 550mg

ABOUT WHITE SAUCE

White sauce, also known as béchamel, is a key ingredient in many French and Italian dishes, and is the base of many other sauces, including mornay sauce, which has the addition of cheese. The consistency of the sauce for this lasagne recipe is medium-thick. If you want a thinner sauce, use 30g (1oz) each of butter and flour, or for a thicker consistency use 50g (1¾oz) of each.

Method

1 Preheat the oven to 190°C (fan 170°C/375°F/Gas 5). Grease a baking dish measuring about 25 x 20cm (10 x 8in) and 5cm (2in) deep.

2 Make the white sauce as shown below. Pour one-third of the Bolognese sauce in the bottom of the dish, then one-third of the white sauce over the Bolognese. Sprinkle with one-third of the cheese. Cover with a layer of lasagne sheets, not overlapping them.

3 Repeat the layers of Bolognese sauce, white sauce, cheese, and lasagne sheets, then repeat the layers once more, finishing with the cheese. Bake the lasagne for about 30 minutes, or until bubbling and golden brown.

Make a smooth, creamy white sauce

1 Melt the butter in a pan placed over a medium heat until it has melted and is foaming. Sprinkle in the flour.

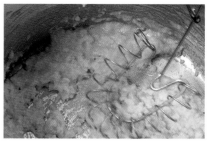

2 Using a hand whisk, whisk the mixture (or "roux") for 1–2 minutes. Remove the pan from the heat.

3 Gradually add the hot milk, whisking constantly. Return to a medium heat and whisk until boiling and thickened.

4 Check the sauce is smooth and the right consistency, then season with salt, pepper, and nutmeg.

Mary's Secrets of Success

Pasta and Rice

1 **Fresh supermarket pasta** cooks more quickly than dried, but a high-quality dried pasta is best for classic Italian cooking. The best is made in Italy from 100 per cent durum wheat.

2 **Always match the sauce to the pasta.** Long string shapes are best dressed with a thin, olive-oil based sauce, which allows the strands to remain slippery and separate, while long, flat ribbons are usually served with a creamy sauce. Short, tubular pasta is great with rich, bulky sauces and in baked dishes, and filled pasta is best with simple sauces that complement the filling without overwhelming it.

Cooking penne, p186

3 **The golden rules for cooking pasta** are to use a large saucepan, plenty of water, and add lots of salt once the water has come to the boil. Don't skimp on the salt. As a guide, use about 1 litre (1¾ pints) water and 1 teaspoon salt per 100g (3½oz) pasta.

4 **To test pasta for doneness,** I always lift out a piece and bite it – it should be tender but still a little firm. The Italians call this *al dente*, literally "to the tooth".

Meat Lasagne, pp190–91

5 Drain pasta thoroughly, particularly hollow shapes like penne, rigatoni, and conchiglie (shells), which trap water. Always dress the pasta as soon as it is drained; it must not be allowed to dry out.

6 If you're going to use cooked pasta in a baked dish, undercook it slightly before mixing it with sauce to prevent it being overcooked in the oven.

7 Italians often splash a ladleful of the pasta water into their sauce; the starch in the water helps the sauce cling to the pasta.

8 When cooking rice, I always find a measuring jug is the easiest and most accurate way to gauge quantities.

9 Long-grain rice (including basmati) should be rinsed well before and after boiling, to remove starch that causes stickiness. Rinse in cold water before cooking, and boiling water afterwards.

10 Rice should be eaten on the day of cooking, as it is susceptible to toxins that cause food poisoning.

Paella, pp200–201

Vegetarian Lasagne

This makes a real change from the classic lasagne and is well worth trying. If I'm having a party I often serve both a vegetarian and meat lasagne, and they're equally popular. For variety, replace some of the mushrooms with butternut squash.

Ingredients

Serves 4

butter, for greasing
500g (1lb 2oz) frozen leaf spinach, thawed and well drained
600ml (1 pint) hot white sauce (see p190)
200g (7oz) Emmental cheese, grated
about 6 sheets no pre-cooking required dried lasagne

FOR THE MUSHROOM SAUCE

2 tbsp olive oil
1 large onion, peeled and chopped
350g (12oz) button mushrooms, trimmed and sliced
2 large garlic cloves, peeled and crushed
40g (1¼oz) plain flour
400g can chopped tomatoes
1 tsp sugar
salt and freshly ground black pepper
1 tbsp shredded fresh basil

PER SERVING

Calories: 668
Saturated fat: 20g
Unsaturated fat: 17g
Sodium: 604mg

Method

1 First make the mushroom sauce: heat the oil in a non-stick sauté pan, add the onion and cook over a medium heat for about 5 minutes, or until just beginning to brown. Add the mushrooms and garlic, stir, then cook for about 5 minutes. Sprinkle in the flour and stir well.

2 Add the tomatoes, sugar, and salt and pepper. Bring to the boil, then reduce the heat and simmer, uncovered, for about 15 minutes or until the sauce has reduced and thickened.

3 Preheat the oven to 190°C (fan 170°C/375°F/Gas 5). Grease a baking dish measuring about 25 x 20cm (10 x 8in) and 5cm (2in) deep.

4 Stir the shredded basil into the mushroom sauce. Spread one-third of the sauce over the bottom of the dish.

5 Scatter one-third of the spinach over the mushroom sauce, using your fingers. Spread one-third of the white sauce over the spinach in the dish, then sprinkle with one-third of the cheese.

6 Cover with a layer of lasagne sheets, not overlapping them. The dish will probably take 3 sheets, but you may have to break them to fit.

7 Repeat the layers of mushroom sauce, spinach, white sauce, cheese, and lasagne sheets, then repeat the layers once more, finishing with the cheese. Bake for about 30 minutes, or until golden brown.

Clean, trim, and slice the mushrooms

1 Wipe mushrooms with a damp cloth to remove any soil (do not wash them). Trim off the stalks with a paring knife.

2 Place each mushroom stalk-side down on a board. Cut downwards into uniform slices with a chef's knife.

Macaroni Cheese with Cherry Tomato Topping

This is the perfect supper dish, which I like to serve with crusty French bread. You can vary the cheese: for example, if you have leftover pieces of Camembert or Brie, freeze them with the skin on, grate when frozen, and add the cheese to the sauce.

Ingredients

Serves 4

30g (1oz) butter, plus
  extra for greasing
200g (7oz) short-cut macaroni
30g (1oz) plain flour
600ml (1 pint) hot milk
115g (4oz) mature Cheddar
  cheese, grated
60g (2oz) Parmesan cheese, grated
1 rounded tsp Dijon mustard
salt and freshly ground black pepper
12 cherry tomatoes, halved
1 tbsp chopped fresh parsley,
  to garnish

PER SERVING

Calories: 543
Saturated fat: 17g
Unsaturated fat: 11g
Sodium: 496mg

Method

1 Preheat the oven to 200°C (fan 180°C/400°F/Gas 6). Lightly grease a medium, shallow baking dish. Cook the macaroni in a pan of boiling salted water for about 10 minutes (or according to packet instructions) until just tender, stirring occasionally. Drain well and set aside.

2 While the macaroni is cooking, melt the butter in a large pan. Sprinkle in the flour and cook, stirring, for 1–2 minutes. Remove the pan from the heat and gradually stir in the milk. Return to the heat, bring to the boil, stirring constantly until the mixture thickens. Lower the heat and simmer for about 4–5 minutes, stirring often, until the sauce is thick and smooth.

3 Remove the sauce from the heat. Mix the two cheeses together. Stir the mustard into the sauce with most of the cheese (reserve a handful for the topping) and the macaroni, then season with salt and pepper.

4 Spoon the macaroni cheese into the baking dish, then scatter over the halved cherry tomatoes and the reserved cheese. Season with pepper. Bake for about 15–20 minutes until golden and bubbling. For a browner topping, finish off quickly under a hot grill. Garnish with parsley.

Grate the cheese

Use the coarse side of a box grater for cheese. The large holes make the job quicker and easier, with less waste.

Prepare the tomatoes

Wash the tomatoes under cold running water, drain well, and cut in half. Make sure they are totally dry before using.

Mushroom Risotto

Risotto is the sort of weekday meal that you can buy the ingredients for on your way home and have on the table within 40 minutes. If you like a bit of colour with the rice, add a few frozen peas towards the end, as you stir in the last of the stock.

Ingredients

Serves 4

10g (¼oz) dried porcini mushrooms

50g (1¾oz) butter

1 small onion, peeled and finely chopped

2 garlic cloves, peeled and finely chopped

1 tsp finely chopped fresh rosemary, plus extra to garnish

250g (9oz) chestnut mushrooms, sliced

300g (10oz) Italian risotto rice, such as Arborio

150ml (5fl oz) white wine

about 1.2 litres (2 pints) hot vegetable stock (see p30)

90g (3oz) Parmesan cheese, grated, plus extra to serve

salt and freshly ground black pepper

handful of rocket leaves, to garnish

PER SERVING

Calories: 567
Saturated fat: 11g
Unsaturated fat: 7g
Sodium: 583mg

TIPS FOR PERFECT RISOTTO

Stir the risotto constantly to give a creamy, moist consistency. To test whether the risotto is done, bite into a grain of rice: it should be tender but still have a bit of firmness to it.

Method

1 Soak the porcini as shown below. Meanwhile, melt the butter in a large, wide pan or deep sauté pan, add the onion, garlic, rosemary, and chestnut mushrooms and cook gently over a medium heat for 4–5 minutes, stirring occasionally, until the onion and mushrooms are soft but not brown.

2 Stir in the rice so all the grains are coated and cook, stirring, for 1–1½ minutes. Raise the heat slightly, then pour in the wine and keep stirring until it has all evaporated. Coarsely chop the porcini and add them, with their soaking liquid, to the rice. Stir again until most of the liquid has gone.

3 Pour in a ladleful of the hot stock and cook gently, stirring constantly, until the stock has been absorbed. Continue to pour in the stock, a ladleful at a time, letting it be absorbed each time before you add any more. Repeat until most (if not all) of the stock has been used and the rice is just tender. This will take 18–20 minutes.

4 Remove the pan from the heat. Stir in the cheese, season to taste, and set aside, covered, for 2–3 minutes. If you have some stock left, pour a spoonful over the surface to keep the risotto moist.

5 Gently stir, then serve sprinkled with some cheese, a grinding of pepper, a little finely chopped rosemary, and some rocket leaves.

Soak the porcini

Put the porcini into 150ml (5fl oz) boiling water. Leave to soak for 15–20 minutes then strain, reserving the soaking liquid.

Simmer the stock

To ensure the stock remains hot all the time while you are adding it to the rice, pour it all into a large pan and keep it bubbling on a very low heat.

Paella

The traditional mix of chicken, seafood, and chorizo works really well in this Spanish dish. Paella rice, which has a slightly chewy texture, is Spain's equivalent of Italy's risotto rice. If you don't have it, Arborio rice makes a good substitute.

Ingredients

Serves 4

large pinch of saffron threads
about 1 tbsp olive oil
150g (5½oz) chorizo, roughly chopped
2 skinless, boneless chicken breasts,
    cut into 5cm (2in) pieces
2 skinless, boneless chicken thighs,
    cut into 5cm (2in) pieces
1 onion, peeled and chopped
2 garlic cloves, peeled and
    finely chopped
1 red pepper, halved, deseeded,
    and chopped
1 tsp paprika
350g (12oz) paella rice
900ml (1½ pints) hot chicken stock
    (see p126)
3 tomatoes, skinned, deseeded,
    and roughly chopped
85g (3oz) frozen peas
150g (5½oz) whole cooked prawns
    with shells and heads
300g (10oz) live mussels, cleaned
salt and freshly ground black pepper
handful of chopped fresh flat-leaf
    parsley, to serve
lemon wedges, to serve

PER SERVING

Calories: 688
Saturated fat: 5g
Unsaturated fat: 10g
Sodium: 824mg

Method

1 Soak the saffron in 2 tablespoons of hot water for at least 10 minutes. Meanwhile, heat the oil in a paella pan or large, deep non-stick frying or sauté pan. Add the chorizo and fry for 2–3 minutes until crisp. Remove with a slotted spoon, drain on kitchen paper, and set aside.

2 Put the chicken in the pan with the oil from the chorizo and cook over a medium heat for 8–10 minutes until browned all over. Add the onion and garlic and fry for 4–5 minutes until the onion is starting to brown. Stir in the red pepper, paprika, and rice and stir-fry for another minute.

3 Stir in the stock, the saffron with its liquid, and the tomatoes. Bring to the boil, then reduce the heat and simmer, covered, for 12 minutes.

4 Scatter over the peas, prawns, and chorizo (don't stir) and cook for 4–5 minutes, or until the rice is cooked and most of the liquid absorbed. Remove from the heat, keep the pan covered, and leave for 5 minutes.

5 Meanwhile, put the mussels in a large pan with 1cm (½in) of water. Cover tightly and cook, shaking the pan occasionally, for 5 minutes or until the shells open. Drain and throw away any that have not opened.

6 To serve, stir the paella gently and season. Tuck the mussels into the rice, scatter with the parsley, and serve with lemon wedges.

Prepare the mussels

1 Scrub the mussels in cold running water. Rinse away grit and remove barnacles with a small, sharp knife. Discard any mussels that are open.

2 To remove the "beard", pull the dark, stringy piece away from the mussel and discard. Alternatively, use a knife to help prise it from the shell.

Vegetables and Side Dishes

Master Recipe

Roast Mediterranean Vegetables

A colourful mix of roasted vegetables with garlic goes well with roast chicken, slow-roast lamb, and grilled meats. After roasting, the whole garlic cloves become really soft and pulpy and full of flavour. Slip the skins off them before serving, or leave them on and let everyone squeeze out the garlic themselves.

Serves 4   **Prep** 15 mins   **Cook** 35 mins

Ingredients

1 red pepper
1 large onion
½ butternut squash, about
   450g (1lb)
1 large courgette, about
   200g (7oz)
1 aubergine, about 200g (7oz)
8–12 whole garlic cloves,
   skins left on
4 tbsp olive oil
salt and freshly ground
   black pepper
200g (7oz) cherry tomatoes,
   preferably on the vine
60g (2oz) olives, such as kalamata
handful of small fresh basil leaves,
   to serve

Special equipment
A large, shallow roasting tin

PER SERVING
Calories: 214
Saturated fat: 2g
Unsaturated fat: 12.5g
Sodium: 105mg

Cook's notes

Use the right tin
Use the largest tin you have for roasting the vegetables so they aren't overcrowded, and keep them in a single layer, otherwise they will sweat rather than roast.

Other options
Try blanched fennel wedges sprinkled with fresh thyme.

Prepare ahead
You can also serve the vegetables at room temperature, drizzled with a little balsamic vinegar, for a make-ahead, all-year-round salad.

Prepare the vegetables

Prep 15 mins

1 Preheat the oven to 200°C (fan 180°C/400°F/Gas 6). Cut out the stalk and core from the pepper, then twist and pull it out in one piece. Halve the pepper and scrape out the white ribs and seeds. Cut each half in quarters to give you 8 wedges.

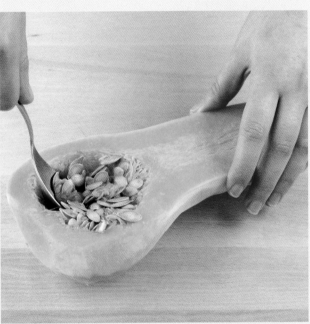

2 Halve the onion lengthways, leaving the root end on. Peel off the skin using a large chef's knife, then cut each half into 4 wedges. Cut off the root ends.

3 For the squash, remove the peel with a small sharp knife. Scoop out any seeds with a spoon and discard. Cut the flesh into chunks about 2cm (¾in) square.

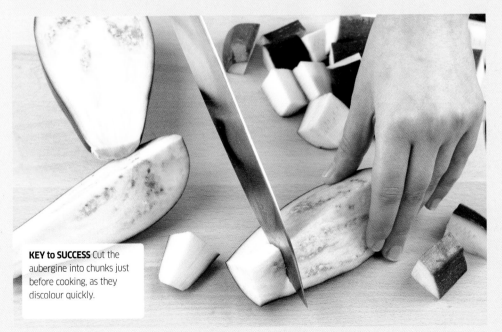

KEY to SUCCESS Cut the aubergine into chunks just before cooking, as they discolour quickly.

4 Trim off both ends from the courgette. Cut the courgette lengthways in half, then cut each half in half again lengthways. Cut across each half widthways into 6, making pieces about 5cm (2in) long. Do the same with the aubergine.

Roast the vegetables

🕐 **Cook** 35 mins

1 Arrange the pieces of pepper, onion, squash, courgette, and aubergine in a large, shallow roasting tin so they are in a single layer rather than piled on top of each other.

2 Scatter over the garlic cloves, drizzle with the olive oil, and toss together so all the vegetables are well coated. Season with salt and pepper.

KEY to SUCCESS Do not add the tomatoes too early or they will become mushy.

3 Roast all the vegetables for about 30 minutes, then add the cherry tomatoes. Turn to coat them in the oil. Return the roasting tin to the oven.

4 Roast for another 5 minutes, or until the vegetables are tender and starting to look charred around the edges. Remove from the oven and scatter with the olives and basil.

"Bursting with flavour, goodness, and summer colour, roasted vegetables are welcome at any time of year."

Potatoes Dauphinoise

Rich and creamy, this is everyone's favourite potato dish. Layer up the potatoes fairly quickly and bake straightaway, otherwise the slices will discolour. If you want to try a lighter version, replace half the cream with chicken stock.

Ingredients

Serves 4–8

butter, for greasing
900g (2lb) large maincrop potatoes,
    such as Maris Piper or Désirée,
    peeled and very thinly sliced
salt and freshly ground black pepper
300ml (10fl oz) double cream
2 large garlic cloves, peeled
    and crushed

PER SERVING

Calories: 561
Saturated fat: 27g
Unsaturated fat: 15g
Sodium: 100mg

USING A MANDOLIN

A mandolin is an extremely useful, sharp-bladed tool that cuts precise, uniform slices and julienne (very fine strips) of various vegetables, including potatoes and carrots. It has adjustable settings, enabling you to select a variety of widths and thicknesses, and is much faster and neater than cutting by hand.

Method

1 Preheat the oven to 200°C (fan 180°C/400°F/Gas 6). Butter a baking dish about 25 x 20cm (10 x 8in) and 5cm (2in) deep. Layer half the potato slices in the dish and sprinkle with salt and pepper. Combine the cream and garlic. Pour half of this mixture evenly over the potatoes.

2 Cover with the remaining potato slices. Sprinkle with salt and pepper, then pour over the rest of the garlic cream. Cover the dish with buttered foil and bake for 30 minutes. Remove the foil and bake for about 50 minutes, or until the potatoes are tender and the top is brown.

Make super-thin potato slices

1 Drag the blade of a vegetable peeler (preferably with a fixed blade) over the surface of the potato in short, sharp strokes to remove the skin.

2 Slide the potato up and down the blade of a mandolin to produce very thin slices. Alternatively, use a food processor or a chef's knife.

Peel and crush the garlic

1 To peel a garlic clove, lightly crush it with the flat side of a chef's knife to loosen the skin (see p52). Peel the skin from the clove with a paring knife.

2 Place the clove in the grille of a garlic press and squeeze the handles together. The flesh will be forced out through the holes in the grille.

Sweet and Sour Red Cabbage

The fruity flavours of sweet and sour red cabbage perfectly complement the richness of goose, duck, and game. Ideally, make it two days ahead as the flavours improve with time. It also freezes very well; just thaw completely before reheating.

Ingredients

Serves 4

900g (2lb) hard red cabbage, cored and coarsely shredded
450g (1lb) dessert apples, peeled, cored, and sliced
250g (9oz) onions, peeled and finely chopped
3 tbsp red or white wine vinegar
4 tbsp redcurrant jelly
¼ tsp ground cinnamon
1 large garlic clove, peeled and crushed
salt and freshly ground black pepper

PER SERVING

Calories: 153
Saturated fat: 0g
Unsaturated fat: 1g
Sodium: 25mg

Method

1 Preheat the oven to 150°C (fan 130°C/300°F/Gas 2). Combine all the ingredients in a large casserole and bring to the boil on the hob over a medium heat, stirring well.

2 Cover and transfer to the oven. Cook for 2–2½ hours, or until the cabbage is very tender, stirring once or twice. Once the cabbage is cooked, either serve it immediately or turn the oven off and leave the pan inside – the cabbage will retain its heat for up to 20 minutes.

Core and slice the apples

1 Peel the apples, then cut them into quarters. Using a paring knife, make a diagonal cut to the centre on each side; remove the cores.

2 Place each apple quarter onto a work surface and cut lengthways into even, crescent-shaped slices with the paring knife.

Core and shred the cabbage

1 Peel off any wilted outside leaves. Use a large chef's knife to cut the cabbage lengthways in half.

2 Cut the cabbage half lengthways in half again. Using a small chef's knife, remove the core from each quarter.

3 Place the cabbage quarter face down and cut across the cabbage to create shreds of the desired thickness.

Minted Peas and Courgettes

These two vegetables make a really interesting mix. By scooping out the courgette seeds and cooking the flesh for the shortest time possible, it keeps the courgettes crunchy and gives them a different look. It is a good way to use cucumber too.

Ingredients

Serves 4

225g (8oz) shelled fresh or frozen
  peas; if fresh, allow about
  400g (14oz) in their pods
2 courgettes, about 400g (14oz)
  in total
salt and freshly ground black pepper
25g (scant 1oz) butter
1 rounded tbsp chopped mint

PER SERVING

Calories: 129
Saturated fat: 4g
Unsaturated fat: 3g
Sodium: 40mg

Method

1 If using fresh peas from the pod, shell them as shown below. Set aside while you prepare the courgettes.

2 Trim the courgettes, then cut them in half lengthways. Scoop out and discard the seeds from the centre of each courgette half as shown below. Slice the courgettes into 1cm (½in) thick pieces.

3 Cook the courgettes in a pan of boiling, salted water for 2 minutes. Tip in the peas, bring back to the boil, and simmer for a further 2–3 minutes, or until they are cooked and the courgettes are just tender.

4 Drain the vegetables well and return to the pan. Add the butter and mint, season, then gently toss together so the butter starts to melt.

VARIATION Minted Peas and Cucumber Instead of the courgettes, use half a skinned cucumber and prepare in the same way. Put in the pan after the peas and heat through for 1 minute.

BUYING AND USING PEAS

If buying peas in their pods, always buy small, young ones. Once picked, they soon lose their sweetness and become starchy. Frozen peas make a great alternative, as they are picked when really young and tender and are frozen immediately, so retain their colour and sweetness. In fact, it is preferable to use frozen peas than older, podded peas. Cook peas for a very short time – just enough to make them tender.

Shell the peas

Press the base of the pod and prise it open, then run your thumb along the inside to release the peas. Put the peas into a bowl while you do the rest.

Deseed the courgettes

Run a teaspoon down the centre of each courgette half to remove the seeds. Make sure you do not take the flesh with it. Discard the seeds.

Mary's Secrets of Success

Vegetables and Side Dishes

Roast Mediterranean Vegetables, pp204–207

1 Try to buy locally grown, seasonal vegetables, or – even better – grow your own. The fresher the vegetables, the better they taste and the more nutritious they are.

2 Store onions, garlic, potatoes, parsnips, swede, and pumpkin in a cool, dark, well-ventilated place. More perishable vegetables, such as peas, sweetcorn, celery, spinach, and ripe tomatoes, should be chilled.

3 When refrigerating vegetables from the supermarket, unwrap them or pierce their bags to prevent moisture build-up.

4 Rinse vegetables thoroughly under running water to remove any excess dirt, and drain well before using.

5 If I'm entertaining, I often prepare vegetables several hours in advance and store them in sealed plastic bags in the fridge. This works fine for most types, except those that discolour quickly (avocados, globe artichokes, celeriac, and Jerusalem artichokes). Potatoes can be peeled and then covered with cold water.

6 Cut vegetables into uniform size and shape where possible to ensure they cook evenly.

7 The microwave is ideal for cooking small quantities of vegetables: you don't need to use much water, which means the vegetables retain their nutrients, colours, and flavours.

Pak Choi and Spring Onion Stir-fry, pp218-19

8 Most vegetables (except potatoes and very watery vegetables, like cucumber and tomatoes) freeze well, although generally they're not quite as good as fresh. Before freezing, blanch them in boiling water, then cool quickly in ice water; this will set the fresh colour. They last 6–12 months and can be cooked from frozen.

9 All pulses (except lentils) need soaking in a bowl of water at room temperature for at least 8 hours before cooking. Alternatively, speed up the process by boiling for 3 minutes, then covering and soaking for 1–2 hours.

10 Boil pulses rapidly for 10–15 minutes at the start of cooking to remove any toxins, then reduce the heat to cook at a simmer (chickpeas, lentils, and split peas don't need the hard boil). Add salt at the end of cooking.

Dhal, pp224-25

Ratatouille

This is an ideal dish to make in the height of summer, when all the vegetables ripen to their peak of flavour. We used to salt aubergines to extract the bitter juices, but newer varieties are picked younger and are less bitter, so it is no longer necessary.

Ingredients

Serves 4

4 tbsp olive oil

1 large onion, peeled and sliced

1 large aubergine, sliced into rounds about 1cm (½in) thick

4 small courgettes, about 300g (10oz) in total, sliced into rounds

6 tomatoes, skinned, halved, and deseeded

1 large red pepper, cored, deseeded, and sliced

1 large garlic clove, peeled and crushed

1 tsp sugar

salt and freshly ground black pepper

1 tbsp shredded fresh basil, to garnish

PER SERVING

Calories: 213
Saturated fat: 2g
Unsaturated fat: 14g
Sodium: 13mg

Method

1 Heat the oil in a large non-stick sauté pan. Add the onion and cook over a medium heat for about 10 minutes, or until softened, stirring often.

2 Add the remaining vegetables, garlic, sugar, and salt and pepper. Stir well. Cover the pan and cook over a low heat for about 45 minutes, or until the vegetables are tender but still retain their shape. Stir gently from time to time. At the end of cooking, check the seasoning, adjust to taste, and sprinkle with the shredded basil.

Prepare the red pepper

Cut the pepper in half lengthways, then cut out the stalk and core with a paring knife. Scrape away the white ribs and seeds from both halves.

Shred the basil

Basil has soft leaves, so to prevent bruising, gently roll the leaves together in a cigar shape, then cut crossways into strips with a paring knife.

Skin and deseed the tomatoes

1 Cut out the core and score a cross in the base of each tomato. Immerse the tomato in a pan of boiling water for 8–15 seconds, or until the skin loosens.

2 With a slotted spoon, transfer the tomato to a bowl of cold water. When cool enough to handle, use a paring knife to peel away the loosened skin.

3 Cut each tomato in half and gently squeeze out the seeds over a bowl. Discard the seeds and juices. If required, chop the flesh coarsely.

Pak Choi and Spring Onion Stir-fry

One of the advantages of this dish is that you can prepare the ingredients ahead before quickly stir-frying. Choose pak choi that have a bit of heart. If you like, stir in a splash of hoisin or black bean sauce at the end for extra flavour and richness.

Ingredients

Serves 4

4-6 pak choi
2 garlic cloves
knob of fresh root ginger
8 spring onions, trimmed
85g (3oz) shiitake or
    chestnut mushrooms
1 small fresh red chilli
2 tbsp sunflower or groundnut oil
3-4 tbsp chicken stock (see p126)
    or water
1-2 tbsp dark soy sauce
toasted sesame seeds, to garnish

PER SERVING

Calories: 90
Saturated fat: 0.8g
Unsaturated fat: 5g
Sodium: 427mg

Method

1 Cut the pak choi into quarters, then cut each quarter in half again lengthways to make thin wedges.

2 Peel and chop the garlic finely and peel and chop the ginger to make about 2 teaspoons.

3 Slice the spring onions, as shown below, and halve or quarter the mushrooms, depending on their size. Deseed the chilli (be careful not to get it near your eyes) and cut it into thin strips.

4 Heat the oil in a wok or large frying pan until hot. Add the garlic, ginger, spring onions, and pak choi and stir-fry over a high heat for about 3 minutes, or until the pak choi has started to wilt.

5 Stir in the mushrooms and chilli with the stock or water and stir-fry for a further 2 minutes, or until the pak choi is tender-crisp.

6 Add a splash of soy sauce and sprinkle the vegetables with the toasted sesame seeds. Serve straightaway.

SOY SAUCE

A fermented mixture of soy beans and roasted grains, soy sauce is available in light and dark versions, the darker being aged for a longer period. Light soy sauce is saltier and thinner, while dark tends to be thicker and more syrupy. Either are good for stir-fries, but it's best to use light where you don't want to colour the ingredients and dark for adding richness.

Slice the spring onions

When slicing spring onions into short lengths for stir-fries, always cut them diagonally. Sliced this way they have the largest surface area, so they cook quickly and absorb other flavours.

Toast the sesame seeds

Put a heavy, dry pan over a medium heat. When hot, tip in the sesame seeds and toast for a few minutes. Move the seeds around so they brown evenly and watch that they don't burn.

Vegetable Curry

This mild curry makes a good accompaniment for meat dishes or, for a vegetarian supper, goes really well with dhal (see pp224–25). Serve it when freshly made, with rice. It isn't suitable for freezing, as the vegetables will lose their texture.

Ingredients

Serves 4

750g (1lb 10oz) mixed prepared vegetables, such as cauliflower, potatoes, carrots, leeks, and French beans
3 tbsp sunflower oil
2 onions, peeled and chopped
1 large garlic clove, peeled and crushed
2.5cm (1in) piece of fresh root ginger, peeled and finely chopped
1 tbsp garam masala
400g can chopped tomatoes
400g can chickpeas, drained
175ml (6fl oz) pineapple juice
salt

PER SERVING

Calories: 247
Saturated fat: 2g
Unsaturated fat: 11g
Sodium: 64mg

Method

1 Cut the vegetables into pieces that are roughly similar in size so they cook evenly. Heat the oil in a medium pan. Add the onions and fry over a medium heat for 10 minutes, or until browned, stirring often.

2 Add the garlic, ginger, garam masala, tomatoes, chickpeas, pineapple juice, and salt and bring to a simmer, stirring. Add all of the prepared vegetables, cover, and cook over a low heat for 15 minutes or until just tender. Check the seasoning and serve straightaway.

Dice the potatoes

1 Place the peeled potato on a firm work surface. Holding it steady with one hand, use a chef's knife to cut it into slices about 1cm (½in) thick.

2 Stack the potato slices, about 3 at a time, and cut the potato vertically into slices of medium thickness. Cut across the slices to produce dice.

Peel and chop the ginger

1 Hold the ginger root firmly in one hand. Using a chef's knife, trim off any knobs and scrape off the skin. You can also use a vegetable peeler.

2 Slice the root, cutting across the fibrous grain to produce fine discs. Stack the discs, press down firmly and shred them into thin slivers.

3 Line up the slivers and cut across them to produce very small dice. For an even finer cut, mound and chop the diced ginger as with herbs.

I like simple, uncomplicated meals. The main thing is that ingredients must be fresh, well prepared, and properly cooked.

Dhal

This is the essential accompaniment for curries. The slightly crunchy topping of lightly fried tomatoes and onions gives an interesting texture contrast to the soft dhal. Lentils contain lots of protein, so are especially good for a vegetarian diet.

Ingredients

Serves 4

250g (9oz) red lentils
2.5cm (1in) piece of fresh root ginger, peeled and grated
1 large garlic clove, peeled and crushed
1 tsp ground turmeric
1 tsp salt

FOR THE TOPPING

2 tbsp sunflower oil
1 tomato, cut into 8 wedges
1 onion, peeled and sliced
½ tsp dried chilli flakes
fresh coriander leaves, to garnish

PER SERVING

Calories: 283
Saturated fat: 1g
Unsaturated fat: 7g
Sodium: 613mg

Method

1 Rinse the lentils as shown below, then put them in a medium pan with 600ml (1 pint) water, along with the ginger, garlic, turmeric, and salt.

2 Bring to the boil, then reduce the heat, and simmer for 20–30 minutes (without covering the pan) until soft.

3 Remove the pan from the heat and mash the lentils with a potato masher. Add a little hot water if the consistency of the mixture seems to be too thick. Keep hot.

4 Make the topping: heat the oil in a sauté pan until hot. Add the tomato wedges, onion, and chilli flakes and stir-fry over a medium heat for about 2 minutes.

5 Transfer the dhal to a serving dish, top with the tomato and onion mixture, and garnish with coriander leaves.

How I prepare and cook lentils

1 Pick over the lentils and remove any shrivelled ones as well as any debris. Place the lentils in a sieve and rinse them under cold running water.

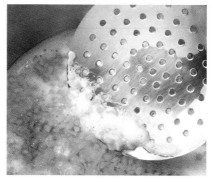

2 Put them in a pan with the other ingredients and bring to the boil. Skim off the scum with a slotted spoon, and cook, uncovered, over a medium heat.

3 After about 20 minutes, check that all the water has been absorbed and the lentils are tender. If they are not ready, cook for another 10 minutes.

Vegetables with Marinated Tofu

On its own, tofu has little flavour, but when marinated it absorbs the flavours of whatever it is cooked with really well. It is made from soya beans, so is a useful source of protein for vegetarians. For added colour, include butternut squash.

Ingredients

Serves 4

500g (1lb 2oz) firm tofu
2 garlic cloves, peeled and
    finely chopped
2 tbsp finely chopped fresh thyme
1 tbsp sesame oil
salt and freshly ground black pepper
1 vegetable stock cube
2 tbsp sunflower oil
2 onions, peeled and thinly sliced
250g (9oz) button mushrooms,
    trimmed and thinly sliced
300g (10oz) cauliflower florets
300g (10oz) broccoli florets
150ml (5fl oz) dry white wine
1 tbsp cornflour

PER SERVING

Calories: 319
Saturated fat: 3g
Unsaturated fat: 15g
Sodium: 447mg

Method

1 Prepare the tofu, as shown below, then cut it into cubes. Place the chopped tofu in a dish. Sprinkle over the garlic, thyme, sesame oil, and salt and pepper. Cover and leave to marinate for 20 minutes.

2 Dissolve the stock cube in 150ml (5fl oz) boiling water. Heat a wok over a high heat for 1–2 minutes until very hot. Add the tofu together with its marinade and stir-fry over a medium heat until lightly browned. Transfer to a plate and keep warm.

3 Heat the sunflower oil in the wok, add the onions, and stir-fry for 3–4 minutes. Add the mushrooms, stir-fry for about 2 minutes, then add the cauliflower and broccoli florets and stir-fry for 2 minutes. Pour in the wine and stock.

4 Blend the cornflour with 2 tablespoons water, then make up to 100ml (3½fl oz) with more water. Pour into the wok, bring to the boil, and stir-fry until the vegetables are tender. Add salt and pepper, then sprinkle the tofu over the top.

VARIATION **Vegetables with Marinated Steak** Substitute 2 fillet steaks (total weight about 300g/10oz) for the tofu and a beef stock cube for the vegetable stock cube. Cut the steaks into thin strips across the grain and stir-fry for 2–3 minutes.

Prepare the tofu for stir-frying

1 Rinse the tofu under cold running water, then place in a sieve or colander until thoroughly drained.

2 Place the tofu on a sheet of kitchen paper and dab it dry to remove any excess moisture before cooking.

3 Set the tofu on the chopping board. Using a large chef's knife, cut it into strips, then across into cubes.

Yorkshire Puddings

I like to make these a day ahead so the oven is free for roasting the beef. Keep them in the same tin and reheat in a hot oven for about 15 minutes. This mixture also fits a 23 x 33cm (9 x 13in) roasting tin, in which case bake for 20–30 minutes.

Ingredients

Serves 6

1 tbsp olive oil or goose fat
salt and freshly ground black pepper

FOR THE BATTER

125g (4½oz) plain flour
2 large eggs
1 large egg yolk
250ml (9fl oz) milk

PER SERVING

Calories: 270
Saturated fat: 6g
Unsaturated fat: 8g
Sodium: 80mg

Method

1 To make the batter, measure the flour into a large mixing bowl and add the eggs and the additional egg yolk, as shown in step 1 (below). Add the milk gradually, as shown in steps 2 and 3, until the batter is smooth, then add the salt and pepper.

2 If time allows, cover the bowl containing the batter with a clean tea towel and let stand for about 30 minutes; this is so the starch grains in the flour absorb the liquid and swell.

3 Preheat the oven to 220°C (fan 200°C/425°F/Gas 7). Place a little oil or goose fat in each hollow of a 12-hole Yorkshire pudding tin and heat in the oven for 10 minutes, or until the fat is melted and very hot.

4 Remove the tin, give the batter a stir, and pour it into the hollows. Return the tin to the oven straightaway, and cook for about 15 minutes until the puddings are well risen, golden, and crisp. Serve immediately.

How I make batter for Yorkshire puddings and pancakes

1 Make a well in the centre of the flour using the back of a tablespoon. Crack the eggs, plus the extra yolk for Yorkshire puddings (but not pancakes), one at a time into the hollow.

2 Add a little milk and whisk gently. As the mixture becomes stiff, add more milk, again a little at a time. Using a spatula, draw in the flour from around the sides of the bowl.

3 Continue adding the remaining milk until the flour is thoroughly blended and the mixture is completely smooth. Add the salt and pepper and whisk once more to combine.

Cauliflower and Leek Cheese

This goes well with roasts, chops, and sausages, or makes a lovely light supper, perhaps with carrots and butternut squash added. Don't over-boil the vegetables; they should still have a bit of bite, as they will cook a little more in the oven.

Ingredients

Serves 4

1 large cauliflower
3 large leeks
30g (1oz) mature Cheddar cheese

FOR THE SAUCE

60g (2oz) butter, plus extra
  for greasing
60g (2oz) plain flour
600ml (1 pint) milk
60g (2oz) Parmesan cheese, grated
60g (2oz) mature Cheddar
  cheese, grated
2 tsp grainy mustard
salt and freshly ground black pepper

PER SERVING

Calories: 484
Saturated fat: 19.5g
Unsaturated fat: 13g
Sodium: 536mg

Method

1 Prepare the cauliflower and the leeks as shown below. Bring a pan of salted water to the boil, add the cauliflower florets and reserved stems, bring back to the boil and simmer for about 4 minutes, or until the cauliflower is just cooked but still has bite. Drain and rinse under cold running water, then drain again.

2 Cook and cool the sliced leeks in the same way (like the cauliflower, the leeks should not be too soft).

3 Grease a shallow baking dish. Preheat the oven to 200°C (fan 180°C/400°F/Gas 6). Arrange the leeks and cauliflower in the dish, with the cauliflower stalks at the bottom and the florets facing upwards.

4 Make a white sauce using the quantities of butter, flour, and milk given here and the method shown on p190.

5 Remove the sauce from the heat and stir in the Parmesan and Cheddar, then the mustard, and season with salt and pepper.

6 Pour the sauce over the vegetables and scatter over the 30g (1oz) Cheddar. Bake for 20–25 minutes, or until golden and bubbling.

Cut the cauliflower into florets

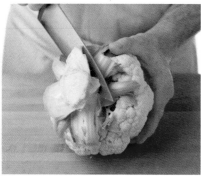

1 Lay the cauliflower on a cutting board with the stalk facing up. Using a chef's knife, trim off the thick main stalk and remove any leaves. Discard.

2 Using a small paring knife, carefully cut the florets from the centre. Cut off any thin, tender stalks and reserve. Rinse with cold water and drain.

Prepare the leeks

Trim and discard any tough outer leaves and the root ends. Cut the leeks crossways into 2.5cm (1in) slices, rinse under cold running water, and drain.

Salads

Master Recipe

Caesar Salad

This classic American salad makes a delicious light lunch, starter, or side salad. A traditional Caesar salad includes a raw or coddled egg, but here I've used mayonnaise in the dressing instead to give a creamy consistency. Other variations include adding fried pieces of crispy bacon, strips of grilled chicken, or flaked cooked salmon.

Serves 4–6   **Prep** 15–20 mins   **Cook** 5 mins

Ingredients

2 romaine lettuces, shredded
30g (1oz) rocket leaves
50g can anchovy fillets, drained
    and snipped into pieces (optional)
50g (1¾oz) Parmesan cheese,
    coarsely grated
salt and freshly ground black pepper

FOR THE CROÛTONS

4 thick slices of day-old white
    bread, crusts removed and cut
    into 1cm (½in) cubes
2–4 tbsp sunflower oil

FOR THE DRESSING

100ml (3½fl oz) mayonnaise
    (see p248)
juice of ½ lemon
2 tsp Worcestershire sauce
1 garlic clove, peeled and crushed
1 tbsp olive oil

Special equipment
A large non-stick sauté pan

PER SERVING
Calories: 510
Saturated fat: 8g
Unsaturated fat: 32g
Sodium: 825mg

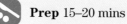

KEY to SUCCESS Drain the croûtons on kitchen paper and leave to cool before adding to the salad.

1 Make the croûtons: place the bread in a plastic bag with the oil and seasoning. Seal the bag and shake well.

2 Place a non-stick sauté pan over a medium heat. When hot, add the bread, stirring, until golden all over.

KEY to SUCCESS Toss the salad well to mix all the ingredients together and serve immediately.

3 Whisk together all the dressing ingredients except the oil. Stir in the oil gradually. Add the seasoning.

4 In a large bowl combine the leaves, anchovies (if using), croûtons, and cheese. Pour over the dressing.

"I love the salty piquancy of the anchovies in this salad, but it is still delicious without them."

Mixed Leaf Salad

This is a lovely way to be able to prepare a salad ahead and keep it fresh. I marinate the firmer vegetables in the dressing in the bottom of the bowl, then lay the delicate salad leaves on top and refrigerate it until needed. Toss the salad just before serving.

Ingredients

Serves 4–6

4–6 spring onions, trimmed
6 celery sticks, trimmed
1 small fennel bulb, trimmed
4–6 tbsp French dressing
½ cucumber
200g packet mixed salad leaves
1 Little Gem lettuce
about 20 leaves of rocket, baby
   spinach, or lamb's lettuce
salt and freshly ground black pepper

FOR THE DRESSING
(Makes enough for 2 salads)

2 tbsp white wine vinegar
2 tsp Dijon mustard
1–2 tsp caster sugar
6 tbsp extra virgin olive oil
1 tbsp chopped leafy fresh herbs, such
   as tarragon, basil, and parsley

PER SERVING

Calories: 148
Saturated fat: 2g
Unsaturated fat: 11g
Sodium: 109mg

ABOUT FRENCH DRESSING

Also known as vinaigrette, this classic salad dressing is very quick and easy to make. It will keep in the refrigerator for up to 1 week, so it's worth making a large batch. Store it in a screw-top jar and shake to re-mix before using. For a really good flavour, use the best extra virgin olive oil and a good wine vinegar.

Method

1 Finely slice the spring onions, celery, and fennel and place in a large salad bowl. Add the dressing and toss well.

2 Cut the cucumber lengthways in half, then cut across into thick slices. Tear all the leaves into manageable-size pieces.

3 Place half the cucumber and half the leaves in the bowl. Add salt and pepper, then the remaining cucumber and leaves. Season again. Cover and chill for up to 4 hours. Combine all the ingredients before serving.

How I make French dressing

1 Place the vinegar, mustard, 1 teaspoon sugar, and salt and pepper into a bowl. Use a hand whisk to combine.

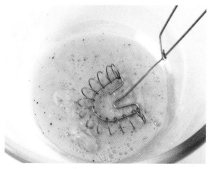

2 Continue whisking the mixture vigorously until the ingredients are evenly combined and thick.

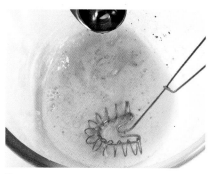

3 Add the oil slowly in a thin, steady stream, whisking vigorously until it is all incorporated.

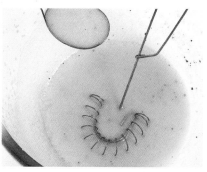

4 Taste the dressing, and add more sugar and salt and pepper, if you like. Stir in the herbs just before serving.

Classic Potato Salad

It is well worth taking the trouble to make this the French way, by tossing the cooked potatoes in the dressing while still warm. I like to add chopped gherkins or sweet cucumber spears for extra crunch and flavour.

Ingredients

Serves 4

550g (1¼lb) new potatoes, such as salad or Charlotte potatoes, scrubbed
salt and freshly ground black pepper
3 tbsp olive oil
1 tbsp white wine vinegar
1½ tsp lemon juice
1½ tsp Dijon mustard
pinch of sugar
5 spring onions, trimmed and thinly sliced
25g (scant 1oz) gherkins, drained and finely chopped
1 tbsp chopped fresh tarragon, plus extra to garnish
1 tbsp snipped fresh chives, plus extra to garnish
6 tbsp mayonnaise (see p248)

PER SERVING

Calories: 336
Saturated fat: 4g
Unsaturated fat: 22g
Sodium: 220mg

Method

1 Put the whole new potatoes in a large pan of boiling, salted water, bring back to the boil, and simmer for 12–15 minutes until just tender.

2 Meanwhile, put the oil, vinegar, lemon juice, mustard, sugar, and salt and pepper to taste into a screw-topped jar. Shake until combined.

3 Drain the cooked potatoes in a colander. Leave briefly until cool enough to handle, then cut them in half.

4 Transfer the potatoes to a serving bowl and, while they are still warm, toss with the dressing. Leave to cool.

5 Stir the spring onions, gherkins, tarragon, and chives into the cold potatoes. Mix gently until everything is well coated with the dressing, then season with salt and pepper. Cover and chill for about 1 hour.

6 Gently stir in the mayonnaise, check for seasoning, and serve scattered with a few more chives and tarragon.

Scrub the potatoes

Wash unpeeled potatoes in water and lightly rub the outer surfaces with a small vegetable brush to remove any dirt. Be careful not to tear the skin.

Chop the tarragon

Strip the tarragon leaves from the stalks, pulling gently to prevent bruising. Chop most of the leaves finely, but reserve a few for garnish.

Tricolore

This flexible salad makes a delicious and decorative first course or light lunch. It is also ideal for serving with other salads or cold meats at a summer party. For added crunch, you could scatter the salad with toasted pine nuts.

Ingredients

Serves 4

3 tbsp olive oil

1 tbsp lemon juice, plus 2 tsp for sprinkling

2 tbsp fresh basil pesto (see p38)

1 ripe avocado

salt and freshly ground black pepper

4 large ripe tomatoes (room temperature), thinly sliced

2 x 125g balls of buffalo mozzarella cheese, drained and thinly sliced

handful of fresh basil leaves, to garnish

PER SERVING

Calories: 366
Saturated fat: 12g
Unsaturated fat: 20.5g
Sodium: 259mg

Method

1 Mix the olive oil and 1 tablespoon of the lemon juice together in a small bowl, then stir in the pesto. Set aside.

2 Remove the stone from the avocado and peel off the skin, as shown below. Cut the avocado into thin slices. Sprinkle with the remaining 2 teaspoons of lemon juice to prevent discoloration. Season with pepper.

3 Arrange the tomato, mozzarella, and avocado slices in rows on a serving plate. Season with salt and pepper. Drizzle the salad with some of the pesto dressing, scatter with basil leaves, and serve with the rest of the dressing.

Prepare the avocado

1 Using a chef's knife, slice the avocado in half lengthways, cutting all the way round the stone.

2 Holding the avocado in both hands, gently twist the cut halves in opposite directions to separate them.

3 Strike the stone with the blade of the knife to pierce it, then lift the stone and prise it off the knife. Discard.

4 Gently scoop out the flesh by sliding a spatula around the inside of the skin, then repeat with the other half.

Four-bean Salad

This is a great salad to have in your repertoire, as most of the ingredients come straight from the storecupboard. Dried beans tend to have a better texture than tinned, but if time is short tinned are fine, provided you rinse and drain them first.

Ingredients

Serves 6–8

125g (4½oz) dried flageolet beans
or 400g can flageolet beans
125g (4½oz) dried cannellini beans
or 400g can cannellini beans
125g (4½oz) dried red kidney beans
or 400g can red kidney beans
125g (4½oz) dried black-eyed beans
or 400g can black-eyed beans
6 tbsp French dressing (see p236)
1 large garlic clove, peeled and crushed
4 celery sticks, trimmed and sliced
1 red onion, peeled and thinly sliced
salt and freshly ground black pepper

PER SERVING

Calories: 458
Saturated fat: 3g
Unsaturated fat: 19g
Sodium: 1402mg

Method

1 Soak the dried beans in cold water for at least 8 hours. Drain and rinse, then cook as shown below, or according to the instructions on the packet. Cook the light- and dark-coloured beans separately, to prevent discoloration.

2 Tip the cooked beans into a colander to drain off most of the water. If using tinned beans, simply put them in a colander and rinse thoroughly under cold running water.

3 Line a baking tray with a double thickness of kitchen paper. Spread the beans on the paper and shake the tray until the beans are no longer wet.

4 Pour the dressing into a large bowl, add the beans, garlic, celery, onion, and salt and pepper and toss well.

5 Cover the salad and chill for about 4 hours. Taste to check the seasoning before serving.

VARIATION Bean Salad with Tuna Drain a 200g can tuna in oil and break the tuna into large chunks. Alternatively, use fresh chargrilled tuna (see p246). Fold the fish into the bean salad before chilling. Garnish with 3 hard-boiled eggs, shelled, cooled, and quartered.

Soak and cook the dried kidney beans

1 Place the beans in a large bowl and cover generously with cold water. Let soak at room temperature for at least 8 hours. Drain and rinse.

2 Place the beans in a pan; cover generously with cold water. Bring to the boil and boil rapidly for 10 minutes.

3 Reduce the heat to low, cover, and simmer gently for 1½–1¾ hours, or until tender. Rinse the beans in cold running water. Drain well.

Mary's Secrets of Success

Salads

Caesar Salad, pp234-35

1 **When planning a salad,** think about the compatibility of the dressing and ingredients. As a general rule, use a plain, delicate vinaigrette to accompany mild flavours, and a stronger dressing for punchier ones.

2 **I like to take advantage of seasonal vegetables** for my salads, such as asparagus or spinach in spring, juicy, vine-ripened tomatoes in summer, fennel in autumn, and coleslaw in winter.

3 **When buying salad leaves,** look for the freshest available. Their colour should be bright and their texture firm and crisp. Try a variety of leaves with different colours and textures.

Tricolore, pp240-41

4 **Always wash salad leaves** to remove grit or soil and to make them crisp. Drain them in a colander and dry well: pat them with a tea towel or kitchen paper, or use a salad spinner.

5 **Salad leaves can be prepared several hours in advance** and kept covered in the fridge, but don't dress them until ready to serve, as they will wilt.

6 Vinaigrette can be kept in a screw-topped jar in the fridge for up to 1 week. Shake well before serving.

7 To avoid bruising delicate leaves, tear them rather than cutting them with a knife. The larger the pieces, the less chance there is of bruising.

Four-bean Salad, pp242-43

Salad Niçoise, pp246-47

8 I like to serve salad as a main meal in summer, particularly for lunch al fresco. Salad niçoise (see pp246–47) or summer couscous (see pp250–51) are great main-course salads and are delicious served with crusty bread.

9 Remember to add fresh herbs to your salads: chives, mint, parsley, basil, and tarragon are all suitable. Edible flowers, such as nasturtiums, add a welcome splash of colour.

10 A wooden bowl and wooden servers are best for salads. Avoid metal bowls and implements, except stainless steel, as they will react with any acidity in the dressing.

Salad Niçoise

For this salad, the tuna steak should be cooked through, whereas often when cooking a tuna steak for a main course it is served very rare (or "blue"). Instead of fresh tuna, you can use a 400g can of tuna in oil, drained and broken into chunks.

Ingredients

Serves 4

2 tuna steaks, each weighing 150g (5½oz)

1 tbsp olive oil

salt and freshly ground black pepper

250g (9oz) baby new potatoes, scrubbed

250g (9oz) French beans, cut in half crossways

1 garlic clove, peeled and crushed

1 tbsp chopped fresh parsley

1 tbsp shredded fresh basil

4 tbsp French dressing (see p236, omitting the mustard)

1 crisp lettuce, such as Little Gem or cos, coarsely shredded

100g (3½oz) cherry tomatoes, halved

4 hard-boiled eggs, shelled, cooled, and cut into wedges

50–75g (1¾–2½oz) black olives in oil, drained

2–3 spring onions, trimmed and thinly sliced

8 anchovy fillets, drained

PER SERVING

Calories: 440
Saturated fat: 5g
Unsaturated fat: 21g
Sodium: 989mg

Method

1 Heat a ridged cast-iron chargrill pan on the hob until hot. Prepare and grill the tuna steaks as shown below. If you do not have a chargrill pan, use a non-stick sauté pan. Set the steaks aside to cool.

2 Cook the potatoes in a pan of salted boiling water for 15–20 minutes, or until tender. Meanwhile, in another pan of salted boiling water, cook the French beans for about 3 minutes. Drain in a colander, rinse with cold water to refresh, then drain again thoroughly.

3 Drain the potatoes and leave them until they are cool enough to handle, then cut into thick slices. Leave to cool completely.

4 Add the garlic, parsley, and basil to the French dressing and whisk to mix. Check the seasoning.

5 Separate the lettuce leaves, then arrange them on 4 individual serving plates. Add the potatoes, beans, tomatoes, eggs, olives, and spring onions, arranging them attractively. Slice the tuna into thick pieces, then lay them on the salad, topped with 2 anchovy fillets per person.

6 Pour over the French dressing. Cover the salad plates loosely with cling film and chill in the fridge for about 1 hour before serving.

Chargrill the tuna steaks

1 While the chargrill or sauté pan is heating on the hob, brush both sides of the tuna steaks with olive oil.

2 Grill or fry for 3 minutes on one side, then turn the tuna over and cook the other side. Season the cooked steaks.

Coleslaw

Home-made coleslaw is the best. I make mine a day ahead so the flavours have time to blend. Some people like the addition of some sultanas, but it's up to you. Keep the leftover mayonnaise in the fridge, tightly covered, for no more than two days.

Ingredients

Serves 4–6

½ white cabbage, about 325g (11oz), cored and shredded
4–6 tbsp French dressing (see p236)
½ small onion, peeled and finely chopped
1 tsp Dijon mustard
salt and freshly ground black pepper
3 celery sticks, thinly sliced
2 carrots, peeled and coarsely grated
150ml (5fl oz) mayonnaise

FOR THE MAYONNAISE
(Makes 200ml/7fl oz)

2 large egg yolks
1 tsp Dijon mustard
salt and freshly ground black pepper
150ml (5fl oz) olive or sunflower oil
2 tsp lemon juice or white wine vinegar
pinch of sugar (optional)

PER SERVING

Calories: 324
Saturated fat: 4g
Unsaturated fat: 26g
Sodium: 125mg

SAVE CURDLED MAYONNAISE

Curdling can occur if the eggs or the oil were too cold when mixed, if too much oil was added, or if it was done too quickly. To save the mayonnaise, add 1 tablespoon hot water and beat well. Alternatively, start again with a fresh egg yolk and oil and slowly add the curdled mixture once the eggs and oil thicken.

Method

1 Place the cabbage in a large bowl and add the French dressing, onion, mustard, and salt and pepper. Toss to mix. Cover tightly and chill in the fridge for about 8 hours.

2 Make the mayonnaise as shown below, bringing all the ingredients to room temperature first. Make sure you add the oil very slowly.

3 Add the celery and carrots to the cabbage, toss to mix, then add the mayonnaise and stir to combine. Cover tightly and chill for 1 hour. Check the seasoning before serving.

Traditional mayonnaise

1 Place the yolks, mustard, and salt and pepper into a bowl and whisk until the yolks have thickened slightly.

2 Add the oil, a drop at a time at first, whisking until thick. Stir in the lemon juice or vinegar and sugar, if desired.

Mayonnaise the quick way

1 Into a food processor fitted with the metal blade put the yolks, mustard, and seasoning; process until blended.

2 With the blades turning, add the oil in a slow, steady trickle. Add the lemon juice or vinegar and sugar, to taste.

Summer Couscous

For this salad, the tiny couscous grains take their flavour from the vegetables, herbs, and seasonings they are mixed with. It is quick and easy to prepare for a summer lunch or supper and goes really well with a selection of cold meats.

Ingredients

Serves 4–6

400ml (14fl oz) vegetable stock
   (see p30)
150g (5½oz) fresh asparagus, trimmed
   and cut into 2.5cm (1in) lengths
250g (9oz) couscous
salt and freshly ground black pepper
juice of 1 lemon
3 tbsp olive oil
6 spring onions, trimmed and sliced
150g (5½oz) mangetout
50g (1¾oz) pine nuts, toasted
3 tbsp chopped fresh parsley
3 tbsp chopped fresh mint
lemon wedges, to serve

PER SERVING

Calories: 374
Saturated fat: 2g
Unsaturated fat: 19g
Sodium: 432mg

ABOUT MANGETOUT

Like sugarsnaps, mangetout (also called snow peas) are cultivated to be harvested before the peas are fully developed, so they're meant to be eaten with the pod. You may find them easier to eat if you slice them diagonally across rather than serving them whole.

Method

1 Heat the stock in a pan and bring to the boil. Add the asparagus, cover, and cook for 3 minutes.

2 Place the couscous in a large bowl. Set a colander over the bowl and pour in the stock and asparagus. When the stock has drained through, lift off the colander. Add salt and pepper to the couscous and stir well. Cover and set aside to cool.

3 Run cold water over the asparagus to cool it quickly, then drain on kitchen paper so all excess moisture is removed.

4 Add the lemon juice and oil to the couscous and toss to mix. Add the asparagus, spring onions, mangetout, toasted pine nuts, and chopped parsley and mint. Toss well, then check the seasoning. Serve at room temperature, with lemon wedges.

VARIATION Tabbouleh Replace the couscous with the same quantity of fine bulgur wheat.

How I toast pine nuts

Spread the pine nuts in a single layer on a baking sheet. Roast in the oven at 190°C (fan 170°C/375°F/Gas 5) for about 10 minutes, shaking halfway, until golden brown. Alternatively, toast them as for sesame seeds (see p218).

Puddings

Double-crust Apple Pie

Homely and traditional, apple pie is the perfect dessert for a special meal. It never fails to please and is surprisingly easy to master. The trick is to have crisp, golden pastry on the outside and tender, juicy fruit that holds its shape on the inside. For crisp, light pastry always work in a cool kitchen with cool ingredients and tools.

Serves 6   **Prep** 45 mins, plus 30 mins chilling   **Cook** 40–50 mins

Ingredients

350g (12oz) plain flour, plus extra for dusting
175g (6oz) hard block margarine, plus extra for greasing
about 6 tbsp cold water
1kg (2¼lb) dessert or cooking apples
juice of 1 small lemon
85g (3oz) sugar, plus 1 tbsp to glaze
1½ tbsp cornflour
1 tbsp milk, to glaze

Special equipment
A 23cm (9in) pie tin and a baking sheet

PER SERVING
Calories: 546
Saturated fat: 11g
Unsaturated fat: 13g
Sodium: 241mg

Cook's notes

Sweetness
Use only the amount of sugar specified and serve extra at the table if necessary, particularly if you've used cooking apples, which are less sweet than dessert apples.

Sugar draws out the juice from fruit, and if there is too much, it may overflow during baking and stick to the bottom of your oven.

Prepare ahead You can keep the pastry, wrapped in cling film, for up to 24 hours in the fridge.

Make and roll out the pastry

Prep 15 mins, plus 30 mins chilling

KEY to SUCCESS Re-wrap the pastry that you're not using immediately in cling film so it doesn't dry out.

KEY to SUCCESS Between each rolling, turn the pastry a quarter turn and dust the rolling pin with flour if sticky. Don't stretch the pastry or turn it over.

1 Make the pastry (see Ingredients and p272), wrap it in cling film, and chill for 30 minutes. Remove half the pastry from the cling film.

2 Flour your work surface and rolling pin. Flatten the pastry. Working from the centre out, roll out the pastry into a circle, about 35cm (14in) across.

Line the pie tin

 Prep 5 mins

KEY to SUCCESS Do not grease the tin before putting in the pastry; it is unnecessary and can cause the pastry to stick.

1 With floured hands, fold the pastry in half, then in half again, to resemble a fan shape. Place it in the tin with the point in the centre. This will help minimize stretching.

2 Unfold the pastry and ease it into the tin without stretching or pulling. Do not worry about the pastry hanging over the edge, because this will be trimmed later.

Make the filling

 Prep 10 mins

KEY to SUCCESS Sprinkling the apple slices with lemon juice helps prevent them browning and adds flavour to the pie.

1 Place a baking sheet in the oven and preheat to 220°C (fan 200°C/425°F/Gas 7). Peel, core, and slice the apples (see p210). Toss in lemon juice, then sugar and cornflour.

2 Turn the apples into the lined tin, then use a fork to distribute the slices, heaping them up towards the centre. Brush the rim of the pastry with a little milk.

Master Recipe

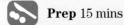

Finish the pie

Prep 15 mins   **Cook** 40–50 mins

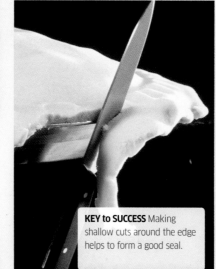

KEY to SUCCESS Making shallow cuts around the edge helps to form a good seal.

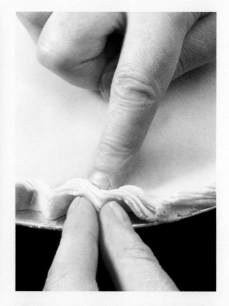

1 Unwrap the remaining piece of pastry, and as before roll it out, fold it into a fan shape and cover the pie.

2 Press down the edges. Trim the excess. Holding a knife horizontally, tap all around the cut edge of the pie.

3 Crimp the edge as shown (see also p273). Brush the top with milk. Cut a 1cm (½in) steam hole in the centre.

KEY to SUCCESS A steam hole allows steam to escape, keeping the pastry crispy.

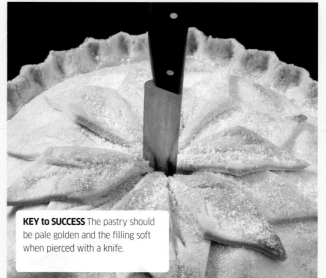

KEY to SUCCESS The pastry should be pale golden and the filling soft when pierced with a knife.

4 Re-roll the trimmings, cut out decorative shapes, and arrange on top of the pie, leaving the steam hole clear. Brush the shapes with milk and sift sugar over the pie.

5 Put the pie on the baking sheet and bake for about 15 minutes, then reduce the oven temperature to 180°C (fan 160°C/350°F/Gas 4) and bake for 30–35 minutes.

"I like to serve my apple pie hot with cream, custard, or a good-quality vanilla ice cream."

Plum Crumble

This is the perfect pudding for a winter's day after Sunday lunch. I sometimes use apricots or blackberry and apple, but the same crumble topping goes well with them all. Just scatter the topping lightly over the fruit to keep it nice and crumbly.

Ingredients

Serves 4–6

750g (1lb 10oz) plums, halved and stoned
45g (1½oz) granulated sugar
2 tbsp water

FOR THE TOPPING

225g (8oz) plain flour
100g (3½oz) butter (room temperature), cut into cubes
45g (1½oz) granulated sugar

PER SERVING

Calories: 680
Saturated fat: 15g
Unsaturated fat: 21g
Sodium: 194mg

PERFECT CRUMBLE

A good crumble contains the right balance of fat to flour and has the texture of fine breadcrumbs. If there is too much fat the topping will melt; if too little the result will be dry. Rub the butter into the flour gently; never mash it with your fingers, and don't make the texture too fine or the topping will be stodgy.

Method

1 Preheat the oven to 180°C (fan 160°C/350°F/Gas 4). Put the plums in a baking dish measuring about 25 x 20cm (10 x 8in) and 5cm (2in) deep. Sprinkle the fruit with the sugar and water.

2 Make the crumble topping: place the flour in a bowl and add the butter. Rub the butter into the flour as shown below, then stir in the sugar.

3 Scatter the crumble topping evenly over the plums. Bake for 45 minutes, or until the topping is golden brown and the fruit juices are bubbling. Test the plums with a skewer to see if they are tender; if not, cover the crumble with foil and bake for a further 10–15 minutes. Serve warm with cream or custard (see p266).

VARIATION Apple Crumble Use 750g (1lb 10oz) cooking apples and 75g (2½oz) sultanas instead of the plums, and light muscovado sugar instead of white sugar. If you like, use half wholemeal and half white flour, or substitute porridge oats or muesli for half the flour.

How I make crumble topping

1 Combine the flour and butter by gently rubbing the butter into the flour using your fingertips. The texture should resemble fine breadcrumbs.

2 Add the sugar to the flour and butter mixture, then spoon the topping over the fruit in an even layer, covering as much of the fruit as possible.

Apple-stuffed Pancakes

These pancakes, filled with apples that are cooked with butter and sugar, make a very naughty, but very special dessert. It is a useful dish when entertaining, as you can prepare it ahead and pop it in the oven just 20 minutes before serving.

Ingredients

Serves 4

65g (2¼oz) unsalted butter, plus extra for greasing
grated zest of 1 lemon
juice of ½ lemon
500g (1lb 2oz) cooking or dessert apples, cored, peeled, and thickly sliced
50g (1¾oz) demerara sugar
sunflower oil, for greasing
8 x 23cm (9in) thin pancakes (see p228 and below)
vanilla ice cream or fresh cream, to serve

PER SERVING

Calories: 336
Saturated fat: 11g
Unsaturated fat: 7g
Sodium: 53mg

Method

1 Make the batter (see p228; it is the same as for Yorkshire Puddings, but omit the additional egg yolk). Let it stand for about 30 minutes.

2 Meanwhile, melt 25g (scant 1oz) of the butter in a large non-stick sauté pan over a low heat. Add the lemon zest and juice, stir to mix, then remove from the heat. Add the apples and coat in the mixture.

3 Return the pan to a low heat, cover, and cook for 5–10 minutes, or until the apples are just tender but still holding their shape. Remove from the heat. Add half the sugar and stir gently. Set aside.

4 Make the pancakes as shown below, ideally using a 23cm (9in) non-stick omelette pan or pancake pan. Before adding the batter each time, heat the pan over a medium heat for 1–2 minutes, then wipe it with a wad of kitchen paper dipped in sunflower oil.

5 Preheat the oven to 200°C (fan 180°C/400°F/Gas 6) and butter a baking dish. Divide the apple filling among the pancakes. Fold the edges of each pancake in over the filling to make a square parcel. Arrange the parcels, seam-side down, in the baking dish.

6 Melt the remaining butter and brush over the pancakes, then sprinkle over the remaining sugar. Bake, uncovered, for 20 minutes, or until piping hot. Serve with vanilla ice cream or fresh cream.

How to make perfect pancakes

1 Grease the hot pan as described in step 4, then ladle in enough batter to cover the base, tilting the pan so that the batter spreads evenly.

2 Cook over a medium heat for 1 minute, or until the pancake is golden underneath. Loosen the edge and flip the pancake over.

3 Cook the other side of the pancake for 30 seconds, or until golden. Slide it onto a plate. Reheat the pan and oil it again before making the next pancake.

Bread and Butter Pudding

You can prepare and assemble this pudding ahead, ideally allowing at least an hour for the milk, cream, and egg to soak into the bread. Then bake it 40 minutes or so before you need it and serve straight from the oven – all puffed up and glorious.

Ingredients

Serves 6

12 thin slices of white bread, crusts removed
about 125g (4½oz) butter (room temperature), plus extra for greasing
175g (6oz) sultanas
grated zest of 2 lemons
125g (4½oz) demerara sugar
300ml (10fl oz) semi-skimmed milk
300ml (10fl oz) double cream
2 large eggs

PER SERVING

Calories: 746
Saturated fat: 29g
Unsaturated fat: 19g
Sodium: 484mg

Method

1 Spread one side of each slice of bread with a thick layer of butter. Cut each slice of bread in half diagonally. Lightly butter a 1.7-litre (3-pint) baking dish and arrange 12 of the triangles, buttered-side down, in the bottom of the dish.

2 Sprinkle over half of the sultanas, lemon zest, and sugar. Top with the remaining bread, buttered-side up. Sprinkle over the remaining sultanas, lemon zest, and sugar.

3 Beat together the milk, cream, and eggs, and strain over the bread. Leave for 1 hour so that the bread can absorb some of the liquid. Meanwhile, preheat the oven to 180°C (fan 160°C/350°F/Gas 4).

4 Bake for about 40 minutes, or until the bread slices on the top of the pudding are golden brown and crisp, and the custard mixture has set completely. Serve at once.

VARIATION Bread and Butter Pudding with Marmalade Spread 6 of the bread slices with thick-cut marmalade after spreading all of them with the butter. Halve the slices, and arrange the buttered ones, buttered-side down, in the dish. Sprinkle with the sultanas, lemon zest, and sugar, then arrange the remaining triangles, marmalade-side up, on top.

Grate the lemon zest

Rub the lemon up and down over the medium grid of a grater, removing just the zest and leaving behind the bitter white pith. Ideally, buy unwaxed lemons for zesting, or wash the fruit first.

Sticky Toffee Pudding with Ginger

Few can resist this enticing combination of spicy ginger pudding with hot sticky toffee sauce. To help with serving, use a fish slice or palette knife to lift the squares from the tin. If it suits you, make the toffee sauce ahead and reheat.

Ingredients

Serves 8

90g (3oz) butter (room temperature), plus extra for greasing
150g (5½oz) light muscovado sugar
2 large eggs
175g (6oz) self-raising flour
1 tsp baking powder
5 pieces of stem ginger in syrup, drained and finely chopped

FOR THE SAUCE

125g (4½oz) butter
175g (6oz) light muscovado sugar
6 tbsp double cream

PER SERVING

Calories: 539
Saturated fat: 19g
Unsaturated fat: 12g
Sodium: 346mg

Method

1 Preheat the oven to 180°C (fan 160°C/350°F/Gas 4). Grease a deep 18cm (7in) square cake tin and line the base with baking parchment.

2 Place the butter and sugar in a large bowl and cream the mixture as shown below. Add the eggs, then the flour and baking powder. Beat well until smooth and thoroughly combined.

3 Stir in the stem ginger, and then 175ml (6fl oz) hot water. Pour the mixture into the tin.

4 Bake in the oven for 45–50 minutes, or until the pudding is well risen, browned on top, and springy to the touch.

5 About 10 minutes before the pudding is ready, make the toffee sauce: place the butter and sugar in a small pan and heat gently, stirring, until the butter has melted and the sugar dissolved. Stir in the cream and heat gently to warm through.

6 Cut the pudding into 8 even-sized squares and transfer to serving plates. Spoon over the toffee sauce and serve at once.

Make the pudding mixture

1 With an electric whisk or a wooden spoon, cream the butter and sugar until light and fluffy. Scrape the bowl's sides to incorporate all the mixture.

2 Drop in the eggs, one at a time, beating after each addition. Add the flour and baking powder and beat until smooth. Stir in the ginger and water.

Traditional English Trifle

Christmas wouldn't be the same without trifle, but it's good at any time of year. If time is short, you can cheat by buying custard, but make sure you use the tinned kind. The custard sold in a carton is delicious, but it's a bit runny for this recipe.

Ingredients

Serves 8

400g can white peach or pear halves
6 trifle sponges
4 tbsp strawberry or raspberry jam
60g (2oz) ratafia biscuits or macaroons
75ml (2½fl oz) medium-dry sherry

FOR THE CUSTARD

300ml (10fl oz) milk
1 vanilla pod, split open
3 large egg yolks
30g (1oz) caster sugar
1 tsp cornflour

FOR THE TOPPING

300ml (10fl oz) double or
  whipping cream
30g (1oz) flaked almonds, toasted,
  to decorate

PER SERVING

Calories: 336
Saturated fat: 11g
Unsaturated fat: 11g
Sodium: 60mg

Method

1 Drain and slice the fruit, reserving 3 tablespoons of juice from the tin. Discard the rest. Cut the trifle sponges in half horizontally and sandwich the halves together with the jam.

2 Line the base of a glass serving bowl with the trifle sponges, and put the fruit and biscuits on top. Drizzle over the sherry and reserved fruit juice, and leave to soak while you make the custard, as shown below.

3 When the custard has cooled slightly, pour it over the sponges, fruit, and biscuits. Cover the surface of the custard with cling film to prevent a skin forming, and chill until set, preferably overnight.

4 Whip the cream until thick, remove the cling film from the custard, and spread the cream over the custard. Scatter the almonds over the top to decorate. Serve chilled.

Make a thick, creamy custard

1 Heat the milk in a pan until hot. Turn off the heat and add the vanilla pod. Cover and infuse for 20 minutes.

2 In a bowl, whisk the egg yolks, sugar, and cornflour until combined. Remove the pod from the milk.

3 Whisk the milk into the egg yolk mixture. Return to the pan and stir over a low heat with a wooden spoon.

4 Cook for about 5 minutes, stirring constantly, until the custard is smooth and coats the back of the spoon.

Summer Pudding

This is the classic summer pudding, but you can use a variety of soft fruit, including blueberries, blackberries, and loganberries, and serve it with extra mixed fruit. I often make double the quantity of this recipe and keep one pudding in the freezer.

Ingredients

Serves 6

8 slices of stale, medium-sliced
   white bread, crusts removed
200g (7oz) strawberries
200g (7oz) redcurrants
200g (7oz) blackcurrants
150g (5½oz) caster sugar
200g (7oz) raspberries
2 tbsp framboise or crème
   de cassis liqueur

PER SERVING

Calories: 235g
Saturated fat: 0.1g
Unsaturated fat: 0.7g
Sodium: 191mg

Method

1 Put 1 slice of bread in the bottom of a 1.2-litre (2-pint) pudding bowl, cutting the bread to fit if necessary, then use 5 slices to line the sides. The slices should fit snugly together.

2 Hull and wash the strawberries, as shown below, and halve them if they are large. Push the redcurrants and blackcurrants off their stalks with a fork. Wash the currants as shown for strawberries.

3 Place the currants in a pan with the sugar and 75ml (2½fl oz) water. Heat gently until the juices begin to run. Stir until the sugar has dissolved, and cook until all the fruit is just tender.

4 Remove the pan from the heat and add the strawberries, raspberries (leave unwashed or they will lose flavour), and liqueur. Spoon the fruit and half of the juice into the bread-lined bowl, reserving the remaining juice. Cover the fruit with the remaining 2 bread slices.

5 Stand the bowl in a shallow dish to catch any juices that may overflow, then put a saucer on top of the bread lid. Place a kitchen weight on top of the saucer. Leave to chill for 8 hours.

6 Invert the pudding onto a serving plate and spoon the reserved juices from the fruit over the top.

Hull and wash the strawberries

1 Pull out the green hull from the top of each fruit, using the tip of a paring knife to help if the hull is difficult to remove. Discard the hull.

2 Rinse in a colander under cold running water as briefly as possible. Shake the colander gently so the fruit does not bruise.

3 Line a tray with a double thickness of kitchen paper. Spread the fruit out on the paper and shake the tray gently so the fruit dries on all sides.

Tropical Fruit Salad

Refreshing and light, this is the perfect dessert to serve after a rich meal. If the fruits you are using are very ripe, you may like to leave out the sugar. Mango is also a great addition, and adds colour, but it must be sufficiently ripe.

Ingredients

Serves 4–6

2 thin-skinned oranges
1 grapefruit
1 small ripe pineapple
1 small ripe melon
1 pomegranate
200g (7oz) seedless black
  grapes, halved
50–75g (1¾–2½oz) caster
  sugar (optional)

PER SERVING
Calories: 247
Saturated fat: 0g
Unsaturated fat: 1g
Sodium: 63mg

Method

1 Peel and segment the oranges as shown below, then segment the grapefruit: cut the fruit crossways in half, work the knife all round the inside, and cut through the white membranes to free the segments. Place the orange and grapefruit segments in a large bowl.

2 Peel, core, and slice the pineapple as shown below. Cut the melon into cubes. Add to the bowl with the citrus fruit.

3 Halve the pomegranate and pick out the seeds. Add them to the bowl together with the grapes. Sprinkle with sugar, if using, and stir gently to mix. Cover and chill for 2 hours before serving.

Segment the oranges

1 Cut the peel from both ends of the orange with a chef's knife. Stand the fruit upright; cut away the peel.

2 Working over a bowl, cut down both sides of each membrane with a paring knife to free segments from the core.

Peel, core, and slice the pineapple

1 Cut off the crown and base. Stand the fruit upright and slice off the skin. Remove as many spikes as possible.

2 Cut the pineapple into quarters lengthways. Cut away the fibrous core from the centre of each quarter.

3 Slice each quarter crossways into chunks. If you like, cut these slices in half to make smaller chunks.

Masterclass

Making Pastry

Once you've mastered the art of pastry-making, you'll be able to create a great range of quiches, tarts, and pies. Keep ingredients and utensils cool, handle the dough as little as possible, and chill it before use or it will shrink in the oven.

Shortcrust pastry

Used for both savoury and sweet tarts and pies (sometimes with sugar added), shortcrust is the most common and versatile type of pastry. For how to roll out pastry and line a pie tin, see pp254–55. For blind baking a pastry case, see p274.

How to make shortcrust pastry

1 Place 350g (12oz) plain flour in a bowl. Cut 175g (6oz) hard block margarine into cubes; add to the flour.

2 Using your fingertips, rub the fat and flour together until you have incorporated all the flour.

3 Continue rubbing in, occasionally shaking the bowl to bring any large pieces of fat to the surface.

4 When all the fat has been rubbed in fully, the mixture will look like fine breadcrumbs.

5 Add about 6 tablespoons cold water, a spoonful at a time. Mix with a knife between each spoonful.

6 Enough water has been added when the mixture just begins to hold together in a soft mass.

7 Gently gather the pastry together against the side of the bowl and turn it out onto the work surface.

8 Gently shape the pastry and pat it into a rough ball. Wrap in cling film and refrigerate for 30 minutes.

Other types of pastry

Puff pastry is often used as a top crust for sweet and savoury pies. Although ready-made is widely available, not all brands are made with butter. Pâte sucrée is easy to make at home, but I suggest you buy filo and strudel pastry.

How to make quick puff pastry

1 Place 250g (9oz) plain flour in a bowl. Add 90g (3oz) each of chilled cubed butter and white vegetable fat. Stir to coat with flour. Add 150ml (5fl oz) cold water. Bind the dough with a knife.

2 Roll out the dough into a rectangle. Fold the bottom third up and the top third down. Press the edges to seal. Wrap and chill for 15 minutes. Place so the folded edges are to the sides.

3 Roll out the dough into a rectangle and fold as before. Turn the dough so the folded edges are to the sides again. Repeat these processes twice more. Wrap and chill for 30 minutes.

Pâte sucrée

A richer pastry than shortcrust pastry, pâte sucrée is used for sweet tarts and tartlets. With your fingertips, blend together 200g (7oz) **plain flour** with 90g (3oz) **butter** (room temperature), 60g (2oz) **caster sugar**, and 3 **egg yolks**, then continue as for shortcrust pastry (see opposite).

PASTRY TIPS

• You can make shortcrust pastry in a food processor: pulse the flour with the fat until the texture resembles that of breadcrumbs, then add the water and pulse again, but only briefly or the pastry will become tough.
• Balls of unbaked pastry dough may be wrapped in cling film and stored in the fridge for a day or two.
• Pastry cases freeze well in their tins. Store baked cases for 4–6 months, unbaked shells for 2–3 months.

Try decorative edgings for pies

 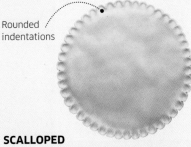 

V-shaped indentations

Rounded indentations

Plait is secured to the pastry rim

CRIMPED
Pinch the outer edge while pushing the inner edge out with the index finger of your other hand (see p256).

SCALLOPED
Press the rim with your forefinger and use a knife tip to indent the dough on each side of your finger.

PLAITED
Cut pastry trimmings into 3 strips and plait together. Moisten the rim with water; press down the braid.

Lemon Tart

This tart takes some time to make, but is well worth the effort. For those who like an even richer, sweeter pastry, you can make pâte sucrée (see p273). If you don't have baking beans, use dried pasta and keep it in a jar so you can use it again.

Ingredients

Serves 8–10

5 large eggs
125ml (4fl oz) double cream
grated zest and juice of 4 lemons
225g (8oz) caster sugar
icing sugar, for dusting

FOR THE PASTRY

250g (9oz) plain flour, plus extra
   for dusting
125g (4½oz) butter (chilled),
   cut into cubes
60g (2oz) caster sugar
1 egg

PER SERVING

Calories: 413
Saturated fat: 12g
Unsaturated fat: 10g
Sodium: 139mg

Method

1 First, make the pastry: put the flour in a large bowl. Add the butter and rub in with your fingertips until the mixture resembles fine breadcrumbs (see p272). Stir in the caster sugar, then bind together with the egg and 1 tablespoon water until the pastry comes together in a ball.

2 Roll out the dough on a lightly floured surface and use to line a shallow 28cm (11in) loose-bottomed fluted tart tin (see pp254–55). Chill in the fridge for 30 minutes. Preheat the oven to 220°C (fan 200°C/425°F/Gas 7).

3 Beat the eggs in a bowl and add the cream, lemon zest and juice, and caster sugar. Stir until smooth.

4 Blind bake the pastry case, as shown below, to ensure the pastry is not soggy. Remove from the oven, let cool, and reduce the temperature to 150°C (fan 130°C/300°F/Gas 2).

5 Pour the lemon mixture into the cooled pastry case. Bake for 35–40 minutes, or until the lemon filling has barely set (it should still wobble a little). Cover the tart loosely with foil if the pastry begins to brown too much. Cool for about 45 minutes, and dust with icing sugar before serving.

6 Leave the tart to cool a little, then dust the surface with icing sugar. Serve warm or at room temperature.

Blind bake the pastry case

1 Preheat the oven to 220°C (fan 200°C/425°F/Gas 7). Prick the pastry base all over with a fork, to prevent air bubbles forming during baking.

2 Line the base and sides with baking parchment and weigh it down with baking beans. Place on a baking sheet and bake for 10 minutes.

3 Remove the beans and paper and bake the empty case for a further 10 minutes, or until the base is lightly browned. Trim the overhanging pastry.

Pineapple and Ginger Pavlova

An impressive party dessert, pavlova never fails to please, and pineapple and ginger make an intriguing blend of flavours. Carefully prise the meringue off the baking parchment after baking; if the pavlova is cooked, the paper will come away cleanly.

Ingredients

Serves 4–6

3 large egg whites (room temperature)

175g (6oz) caster sugar

1 tsp vinegar

1 tsp cornflour

300ml (10fl oz) double or whipping cream

200g can pineapple chunks in natural juice, drained

5 pieces of stem ginger in syrup, drained and finely chopped

PER SERVING

Calories: 513
Saturated fat: 19g
Unsaturated fat: 10g
Sodium: 116mg

WHISKING TIPS

You will get a greater volume when whisking egg whites if the eggs are at room temperature rather than cold, so take them out of the fridge at least 30 minutes before they are needed. Equipment must be scrupulously clean and dry. Once whisked, egg whites need to be used at once.

Method

1 Preheat the oven to 150°C (fan 130°C/300°F/Gas 2). Line a baking sheet with baking parchment and mark a 20cm (8in) circle on it.

2 Whisk the egg whites until they stand in stiff peaks, as shown below, then add the sugar, 1 teaspoon at a time, continuing to whisk on full speed until the whites are glossy. Blend the vinegar and cornflour together and whisk into the whites with the last spoonful of sugar.

3 Spoon the meringue onto the circle on the paper, and spread it so that the edge is slightly higher than the centre. Place the meringue in the oven and bake for 1 hour.

4 Remove the baking parchment, turn off the oven, and return the meringue to the oven on its baking sheet. It will cool as the oven cools.

5 Transfer the meringue to a platter. Whip the cream until thick, put it in the centre of the meringue, and top with the pineapple and ginger.

VARIATION Summer Fruit Pavlova Replace the pineapple and ginger with soft summer fruits, for instance strawberries, raspberries, and blueberries.

Whisk the egg whites to stiff peaks

1 Place the egg whites in a large bowl. Using an electric mixer on full speed, begin whisking, moving the beaters around the bowl.

2 Continue whisking the egg whites on full speed, still moving the beaters around the bowl, until the whites stand in stiff peaks. Use immediately.

Meringues with Raspberry Coulis

The meringues can be made ahead and will keep in an airtight tin for up to one month. Sandwich them together at the last minute, as the cream will make them go soft. The coulis is good for other desserts too, especially spooned over ice cream.

Ingredients

Serves 4

2 egg whites (room temperature)
100g (3½oz) caster sugar
450ml (15fl oz) double or
  whipping cream
300g (10oz) raspberries, to serve
fresh mint leaves, to decorate

FOR THE COULIS

300g (10oz) raspberries
juice of ½–1 lemon, to taste
icing sugar, to taste

PER SERVING

Calories: 400
Saturated fat: 19g
Unsaturated fat: 10g
Sodium: 55mg

Method

1 First, make the coulis: purée the raspberries (do not wash them, or they will lose flavour) in a food processor fitted with the metal blade. Rub the purée through a sieve to remove the seeds.

2 Add the lemon juice to the raspberry purée, then sweeten to taste with icing sugar. Cover and chill until ready to serve.

3 Preheat the oven to 140°C (fan 120°C/275°F/Gas 1). Make the meringues with the egg whites and sugar, as shown below.

4 Whip the cream until it is thick. Sandwich the meringues together in pairs, with the cream in the middle.

5 Spoon the coulis in a pool on each of the 4 dessert plates. Place a pair of meringues on each pool of sauce. Dust with icing sugar, if desired.

6 Divide the raspberries between the plates, placing them alongside the meringues, and decorate with the fresh mint leaves.

Make beautifully light meringues

1 Place the egg whites in a bowl and whisk with an electric mixer on full speed until stiff. Add the sugar, 1 teaspoon at a time, continuing to whisk until the whites are glossy.

2 Cover a baking sheet with a piece of baking parchment. Place 8 individual dessertspoonfuls of the mixture onto the paper, making attractive swirling patterns with the back of the spoon.

3 Bake for 45 minutes to 1 hour until firm and crisp. Lift one to check that it comes off the paper easily. Leave the meringues to cool slightly, then lift them off with a fish slice.

Mango Passion

This is a very quick and useful, make-ahead dessert. If you wish, add two passion fruits to the mango, or replace the mango with the summer fruits that you would put in a summer pudding (see pp268–69), with an added dash of sugar.

Ingredients

Serves 4

1 large ripe mango
90g (3oz) light muscovado sugar
150g (5½oz) half-fat crème fraîche
150g (5½oz) Greek-style natural yogurt

PER SERVING

Calories: 254
Saturated fat: 6g
Unsaturated fat: 3g
Sodium: 69mg

BUYING MANGOES

It's very important to use mangoes at the right stage of ripeness. Choose fruit that "gives" slightly when gently squeezed and has a perfumed aroma at the stem end. Avoid mushy-looking fruit with black spots, blemishes, or wrinkles. If unripe, leave to ripen in a warm place or in a paper bag. Eat at room temperature.

Method

1 Remove the mango stone and chop the flesh as shown below. Divide it equally among 4 serving glasses or ramekins. Add the juice from the mangoes, then sprinkle each portion with 1 teaspoon sugar.

2 Combine the crème fraîche and yogurt in a small bowl. Spoon the mixture on top of the mango pieces.

3 Sprinkle the remaining sugar evenly over the cream topping. Chill the dessert in the fridge for 2 hours before serving.

VARIATION Orange Passion Instead of the mango, use 3 large, thin-skinned oranges. Peel then slice the fruit crossways into rounds. Divide the orange slices equally among the glasses or ramekins. Continue as in the main recipe.

Destone, slice, and dice the mango

1 Using a chef's knife, cut the fruit vertically along one side of the flat stone. Repeat on the opposite side.

2 Laying the piece with the stone flat-side down, cut away the flesh, working around the stone. Chop into cubes.

3 Using a small sharp knife, score the mango halves in a criss-cross pattern. Cut up to, but not through, the skin.

4 Press the skin to open out the fruit segments, then run a sharp knife close to the skin to remove the flesh.

Mary's Secrets of Success

Puddings

Tropical Fruit Salad, pp270–71

1 **Always use the type of cream** specified in a recipe, as the fat content is often crucial to its success. Never use a low-fat alternative unless it has been suggested.

2 **If you're serving a rich main course,** it's best to opt for a fruit-based dessert. If you're offering a selection of desserts, a fruity one is a must.

3 **Piped whipped cream** adds a professional touch to desserts, and with a little practice this is not difficult to do. Use a piping bag and a nozzle, preferably a star-shaped one.

Chocolate Mocha Mousse, pp286–87

4 **Take care when melting chocolate,** especially white chocolate. Don't allow it to overheat or come into contact with any steam, as this could cause it to scorch or harden.

5 **I often decorate my puddings with chocolate;** it makes a great finishing touch. Simply rub chilled chocolate over the large grid of a grater, or use a vegetable peeler to create long curls from chocolate (it's easier if the chocolate is slightly warm).

6 Chilled desserts can be made well in advance so are great for dinner parties. Fruit salads, trifles, creamy mousses, meringues, and cheesecakes – all can be kept in the fridge or freezer, to be served when you're ready.

Double-crust Apple Pie, pp254-57

7 To get maximum juice from citrus fruits, roll the fruit gently on a worktop, pressing lightly. Or heat in the microwave on a high setting for 30 seconds, just until the fruit feels warm.

8 A little milk, beaten egg, or egg white brushed onto a pastry lid will give an attractive, shiny finish. Sprinkle with sugar for a crisp, sweet glaze.

9 Keep pastry trimmings to make small decorative shapes that you can fix to the edge of a pastry case or arrange on the lid. Cut the shapes freehand or using cutters, and attach them with water.

10 Most puddings – whether hot or cold – freeze well. However, custard-based and milk puddings are not very successful as they tend to separate.

Lemon and Lime Cheesecake

Of all the desserts in this book, this lemon and lime cheesecake is one of the simplest to make. You must use full-fat condensed milk and cream cheese for the recipe to work, as the filling won't set if you use low-fat substitutes.

Ingredients

Serves 4–6

10 digestive biscuits, crushed
50g (1¾oz) butter, melted
25g (scant 1oz) demerara sugar
150ml (5fl oz) double cream
397g can full-fat condensed milk
175g (6oz) full-fat cream cheese
    (room temperature)
grated zest and juice of 2 large lemons
grated zest and juice of 1½ limes
150ml (5fl oz) double or whipping
    cream, to decorate
½ lime, thinly sliced, to decorate

PER SERVING
Calories: 668
Saturated fat: 25g
Unsaturated fat: 16g
Sodium: 471mg

Method

1 First, make the crust: place the crushed biscuits, as shown below, together with the butter and sugar, in a medium bowl and stir until the ingredients are thoroughly mixed.

2 Turn the crust mixture out into a 20cm (8in) loose-bottomed tart tin and press firmly and evenly over the bottom and up the sides using the back of a metal spoon. Chill for 30 minutes until set.

3 Make the filling: place the double cream, condensed milk, and cream cheese in a bowl with the lemon and lime zests. Mix thoroughly. Using a balloon whisk, gradually whisk in the lemon and lime juices and continue whisking until the mixture thickens.

4 Pour the lemon and lime filling into the crumb crust and spread it evenly. Cover and chill overnight.

5 Up to 6 hours before serving, whip the cream, as shown below, until it just holds its shape. Decorate the top of the cheesecake with swirls of whipped cream and slices of lime, then return to the fridge.

Crush the biscuits

Place the biscuits in a clear plastic bag. Lay the bag on a flat surface and run a rolling pin back and forth over the biscuits until they form crumbs.

Whip the cream

1 Put chilled cream into a chilled bowl and start whipping slowly until the cream begins to thicken. (If using an electric mixer, use the lowest speed.)

2 Once the cream has thickened, start whipping a little faster. Lift the whisk to see if the cream retains its shape. If not, continue for a little longer.

Chocolate Mocha Mousse

I like chocolate mousse to be rich in flavour with a light, silky texture, and a hint of coffee makes it extra special. The beauty of a dessert like this is that you can spoon it into individual dishes, pop it in the fridge, and it's all ready to serve when needed.

Ingredients

Serves 4

150g (5½oz) plain dark chocolate
2 large egg yolks
45g (1½oz) caster sugar
150g (5½oz) full-fat crème fraîche
150ml (5fl oz) double or
  whipping cream
1 tsp instant coffee granules
chocolate curls or finely grated
  chocolate, to decorate

PER SERVING

Calories: 551
Saturated fat: 27g
Unsaturated fat: 16g
Sodium: 25mg

Method

1 Break the chocolate into a large heatproof bowl and set it over a pan of gently simmering water, as shown below. The base of the bowl should not touch the water. Leave until just melted, then remove the pan from the heat, stir, and leave the chocolate to cool slightly.

2 Put the egg yolks and sugar in a medium heatproof bowl. Set the bowl over a pan of gently simmering water, as above. Whisk with an electric hand whisk on low speed for 4 minutes, or use a balloon whisk, which will take a little longer.

3 When the mixture has become paler and thicker, remove the bowl from the heat and continue whisking for a further minute. Set aside to cool slightly, stirring occasionally so the mixture does not stiffen. If it does, stir in 1–2 teaspoons of the crème fraîche to slacken.

4 Pour the cream into a medium mixing bowl and sprinkle over the coffee. Whip the cream to soft peaks and fold in the crème fraîche. Fold the cream mixture into the cooled dark chocolate, then fold in the egg yolk mixture. Make sure everything is well combined.

5 Spoon into glasses and chill for 1 hour. Decorate with chocolate curls, as shown below, or finely grated chocolate (using chilled chocolate).

Melt the chocolate

Heat the chocolate gently over a pan of simmering water until just melted. Remove the pan from the heat and stir until smooth and creamy.

Make chocolate curls

To make chocolate curls, simply pull a vegetable peeler along the flat side of a chocolate bar. It works best if the chocolate is slightly warm.

Crème Caramel

This timeless dessert is always better made a day ahead so the caramel has time to soak into the custard. To make sure the sugar doesn't crystallize, don't use a non-stick pan for the caramel and don't stir once the sugar has dissolved.

Ingredients

Makes 6

175g (6oz) granulated sugar
4 eggs
30g (1oz) vanilla sugar
  (see below)
450ml (15fl oz) whole milk
150ml (5fl oz) double cream

PER SERVING

Calories: 366
Saturated fat: 11g
Unsaturated fat: 12g
Sodium: 105mg

MAKING VANILLA SUGAR

You can buy sachets of vanilla sugar or make your own by pushing a split vanilla pod into a jar of caster sugar. After a few days, the sugar will smell and taste of vanilla. If you don't have vanilla sugar, use caster sugar and 1 teaspoon vanilla extract instead.

Method

1 Preheat the oven to 160°C (fan 140°C/325°F/Gas 3). Put the granulated sugar and 8 tablespoons of water in a heavy pan and place over a low heat until the sugar has dissolved. Increase the heat and bring to the boil, and cook without stirring until the caramel is a pale golden colour.

2 Working quickly, pour the hot caramel into 6 small ramekins. Gently swirl the dishes so that the caramel comes about halfway up the sides of each ramekin. Set aside to cool.

3 Meanwhile, make the custard: whisk the eggs and vanilla sugar in a large bowl. Heat the milk and cream in a pan over a medium heat until warm, then pour into the egg mixture in the bowl, stirring well. Strain the custard into a heatproof jug and pour it into the ramekins.

4 Place the ramekins in a roasting tin and add enough hot water to come halfway up the sides of the dishes.

5 Bake for 30–40 minutes until just set and just firm to the touch but not solid. Remove the ramekins from the tin, cool, then chill for 8 hours.

6 Gently pull the edges of the custard away from the sides of each ramekin using a fingertip. Place a serving plate over the top of the ramekin and invert the crème caramel onto the plate.

Fill the ramekins

Once the caramel has cooled and set, pour the strained custard in the jug over the caramel, evenly distributing the mixture between the ramekins.

Cakes and Biscuits

Victoria Sandwich Cake

Once you've baked a cake, you'll never want to buy one again. Not only will a home-baked cake taste fresher and better than a bought one, it will also fill your kitchen with an irresistible aroma. This all-in-one method (where all the ingredients are put into the bowl at the same time and beaten together) is simplicity itself.

 Serves 6   **Prep** 15–20 mins   **Cook** 20–30 mins

Ingredients

225g (8oz) butter (room temperature) or vegetable spread (at least 70% fat), plus extra for greasing
225g (8oz) caster sugar
225g (6oz) self-raising flour
2 level tsp baking powder
4 large eggs

FOR THE FILLING AND TOPPING
about 4 tbsp raspberry or strawberry jam
a little caster sugar, for sprinkling

Special equipment
2 deep 20cm (8in) loose-bottomed, round sandwich tins

PER SERVING
Calories: 511
Saturated fat: 8g
Unsaturated fat: 17g
Sodium: 513mg

Cook's notes

Shopping tips
You can save time by using ready-cut circles of baking parchment, available from specialist cook shops, department stores, and mail-order companies.

Prepare ahead
The cake is best eaten on the day of baking, but it will keep in an airtight container for 1–2 days and can be frozen for up to 3 months: freeze the unfilled layers separately, with the base papers on. Wrap each layer in foil and put in a freezer bag.

Prepare the tins

 Prep 5 mins

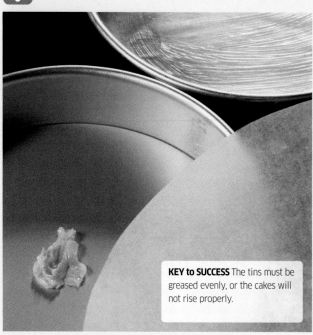

KEY to SUCCESS The tins must be greased evenly, or the cakes will not rise properly.

Preheat the oven to 180°C (fan 160°C/350°F/Gas 4). Cut 2 baking parchment circles, grease the sandwich tins with butter or vegetable spread, and put the circles inside. Grease the circles. (See also p300.)

Make the mixture

 Prep 10 mins

Master Recipe

KEY to SUCCESS
Always use exactly the right amount of baking powder; too much will make the cake dry.

1 Place the butter or vegetable spread in a large bowl, then add the caster sugar, self-raising flour, and baking powder. Crack the eggs one at a time and add to the bowl.

KEY to SUCCESS
Be careful not to over-mix. You can get a good result with a wooden spoon, but it will take a little longer.

2 Using the electric mixer on a slow speed, beat for 2 minutes, or until smooth. The mixture will be soft enough to drop off the beaters when you lift them up.

3 Divide the mixture equally between the prepared cake tins and level the surfaces with a palette knife or spatula, smoothing it over the surface of the two cakes.

Bake and assemble the cake

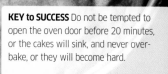 **Prep** 5 mins    **Cook** 20–30 mins

KEY to SUCCESS Do not be tempted to open the oven door before 20 minutes, or the cakes will sink, and never over-bake, or they will become hard.

1 Bake both cakes for 20–30 minutes. When done, they will shrink away from the sides and the tops will spring back if pressed. Cool for 2 minutes; loosen the edges with a knife.

2 After about 10 minutes, push the cakes out of their tins on their bases, invert them onto a thick tea towel, and remove the bases. Cool the cakes the right way up on a rack.

3 Soften the jam with a palette knife. When the cakes are cold, remove the lining papers and invert one cake layer onto a plate. Spread with jam, put the other layer on top, and sprinkle with caster sugar.

"I always use a really good-quality jam, and sometimes I add whipped cream too."

Lemon Drizzle Traybake

An all-time favourite, lemon drizzle traybake is perfect for bake sales, as it cuts neatly, is easy to transport, and keeps well. To ensure the lemon sinks into the mixture, pour over the glaze while the cake is still warm.

Ingredients

Makes 16 slices

225g (8oz) butter (room temperature) or vegetable spread (at least 70% fat), plus extra for greasing

225g (8oz) caster sugar

275g (9½oz) self-raising flour

1 tsp baking powder

4 large eggs

4 tbsp milk

grated zest of 2 lemons

FOR THE GLAZE

juice of 2 lemons

175g (6oz) sugar

PER SERVING

Calories: 297
Saturated fat: 4g
Unsaturated fat: 8g
Sodium: 242mg

Method

1 Preheat the oven to 180°C (fan 160°C/350°F/Gas 4). Grease a traybake tin measuring 30 x 23cm (12 x 9in) and 4cm (1½in) deep and line the base with baking parchment.

2 Place the butter, sugar, flour, baking powder, eggs, milk, and lemon zest in a large bowl. Beat with an electric mixer for 1–2 minutes, or with a wooden spoon for a little longer, until smooth.

3 Turn the mixture into the lined tin and spread evenly. Use a spatula to smooth and scrape up all the mixture around the sides of the bowl.

4 Bake in the preheated oven for 35–40 minutes, or until risen and springy to the touch.

5 Run a knife around the edge of the traybake to loosen it from the tin, then transfer to a wire rack.

6 Make the glaze: mix the lemon juice with the sugar and spoon over the warm cake. Leave to cool, then cut into 16 rectangular slices.

MY LEMON-SQUEEZING TIP

You can get so much more juice out of lemons if they're warm when you squeeze them. To warm them up, cut the lemons in half widthways, pop them in the microwave on a high setting for 30 seconds, then squeeze them as shown here. You will be amazed by how much more juice you will get than if you squeezed them straight from the fridge!

Squeeze the lemon

1 Firmly press half a lemon over a lemon squeezer and twist until all the juice is extracted. If the fruit is warm it will yield more juice.

2 Remove the strainer and discard the pips and pith. If not using immediately, store the lemon juice in a covered container in the fridge.

Vanilla Cupcakes with Swirly Icing

The swirled, two-toned icing makes these pretty cupcakes really distinctive, and you can achieve the effect using a regular piping bag. Have fun experimenting with the huge range of coloured and patterned paper cases and sprinkles available.

Ingredients

Makes 12

175g (6oz) butter (room temperature), cut into large pieces
175g (6oz) self-raising flour
175g (6oz) caster sugar
½ tsp baking powder
3 large eggs
½ tsp vanilla extract

FOR THE ICING

175g (6oz) butter (room temperature), cut into large pieces
½ tsp vanilla extract
2-3 tbsp milk
350g (12oz) icing sugar, sifted
pink edible colouring
edible pink hearts or other sprinkles, to decorate

PER SERVING

Calories: 465
Saturated fat: 16g
Unsaturated fat: 10g
Sodium: 280mg

SWIRLY COLOURED ICING

It's easy to make the colour of the icing too strong. To prevent putting in too much edible colouring, use a cocktail stick to add a drop at a time until you have the shade that you like. Instead of using a regular piping bag, you can buy dual-compartment piping bags, which automatically separate the two colours, allowing you to pipe them at the same time in a similar way.

Method

1 Preheat the oven to 180°C (fan 160°C/350°F/Gas 4). Line a 12-hole muffin tin with paper cupcake or muffin cases.

2 Put all the cake ingredients into a large bowl and beat with an electric hand whisk or a wooden spoon until smooth and evenly mixed. Divide the mixture evenly between the paper cases.

3 Bake for 20–25 minutes, or until the cakes are well risen and firm on top. Transfer to a wire rack to cool.

4 Make the icing: put the butter, vanilla extract, 2 tablespoons of the milk, and half the icing sugar in a large bowl and beat until smooth. Beat in the remaining icing sugar, and pour in the rest of the milk if needed to make the icing the right consistency.

5 Put half of the icing into another bowl and colour it pale pink with the edible colouring. Carefully spoon this down one side of a piping bag fitted with a No. 8 star nozzle, then spoon the non-coloured icing down the other side of the bag. Twist the end of the bag to seal the icing in.

6 Pipe swirls of the icing on top of each cupcake. Scatter with the edible pink hearts, or other sprinkles, to decorate.

Make the cupcake icing

Using an electric or hand whisk, beat the icing ingredients until well mixed. Aim for a soft, fluffy consistency. Add extra milk if the mixture is too dry.

Masterclass

Baking Cakes

If you're new to baking, the main thing to remember is to follow recipes very carefully, make sure you weigh accurately, and use the right equipment. If you follow these simple instructions, you'll achieve perfect results every time.

Preparation and baking

Always use the exact-sized tin specified in the recipe, and take time to prepare the tins properly so the cake doesn't stick. The basic steps for baking a cake are shown below, but see also pp292–94 and pp316–17 for more baking tips.

How to bake a cake

1 Set the tin on a sheet of baking parchment. Mark around the base with a pencil. Cut out the shape.

2 Spread softened butter or margarine over the base and sides using a pastry brush or kitchen paper.

3 Press the parchment shape over the base of the tin. Lightly grease if directed in the recipe.

4 Make the cake mixture as in the recipe, using a hand-held electric mixer or food processor, or by hand.

5 As soon as the mixture is prepared, turn it into the tin, level the surface, and transfer to the oven.

6 To test if the cake is done, lightly press the middle with a fingertip; the cake should spring back.

7 Leave the cake to cool for 2 minutes, then run a knife around the side; cool the right way up on a rack.

8 When the cake is cold, peel off the lining paper. If desired, cut the cake in half with a sharp knife.

Icing, filling, and decorating

Once your cake has cooled, you're ready to add the finishing touches. Don't worry if it looks less than perfect – icing can cover up a multitude of sins, and even simply piped whipped cream can distract the eye from imperfections. Whipped cream, jam, and buttercream make quick and easy fillings.

How to pipe whipped cream

1 Insert your chosen nozzle into a piping bag. You may need to snip the end of the bag to fit the nozzle.

2 Hold the bag in one hand and fold the top of the bag over your hand. Spoon in the whipped cream.

3 When the bag is full, twist the top tightly until there is no air left inside the bag.

4 Hold the bag upright. Gently squeeze the top to pipe the cream in a steady stream, guiding the nozzle.

How to ice a cake

Stand the cooled cake on a wire rack. Using a palette knife, spread the icing with long, smooth strokes over the top and side of the cake. For the top, you can make swirl patterns or leave it smooth, as you like. Carefully slide the iced cake onto a plate.

ICING TIPS

• Place a sheet of greaseproof paper beneath the wire rack; any excess icing will drip onto the paper.
• If icing sticks to the palette knife, dip the knife in warm water to dilute the icing a little.
• Most uncooked icings, such as buttercream, can be made ahead and stored in a tightly covered container.

Try different types of icing

BUTTERCREAM ICING
You can make this icing in a variety of flavours; it is particularly popular for cupcakes (see pp298–99).

FROSTING
With less butter than buttercream, this is a great topping for chocolate brownies (see pp308–309).

GLAZE
A glaze, often flavoured with lemon, is poured over while the cake is still hot (see pp296–97).

Carrot and Walnut Cake with Cream Cheese Icing

For this classic carrot cake recipe, it's important to use full-fat cream cheese for the icing; if you use a low-fat version, the icing will just run off the cake. Carrot cake is beautifully moist, so keeps well. If your kitchen is warm, store the cake in the fridge.

Ingredients

Serves 8

250ml (9fl oz) sunflower oil
4 large eggs
225g (8oz) light muscovado sugar
200g (7oz) carrots, peeled and
    coarsely grated
300g (10oz) self-raising flour
2 tsp baking powder
1 tsp ground mixed spice
1 tsp ground ginger
75g (2½oz) walnuts, shelled and
    chopped, plus 8 halves to decorate

FOR THE ICING

50g (1¾oz) butter (room temperature)
25g (scant 1oz) icing sugar
250g (9oz) full-fat cream cheese
    (room temperature)
a few drops of vanilla extract

PER SERVING

Calories: 765
Saturated fat: 17g
Unsaturated fat: 38g
Sodium: 450mg

Method

1 Preheat the oven to 180°C (fan 160°C/350°F/Gas 4). Grease two deep 20cm (8in) round sandwich tins and line the bases of the cake tins with baking parchment.

2 In a large bowl, combine all the ingredients for the cake mixture as shown below. Spoon the mixture evenly between the tins.

3 Put the cakes in the oven and bake for about 35 minutes, or until golden brown, risen, and shrinking away from the sides of the tins. Transfer to a wire rack to cool.

4 Make the icing: measure the butter, icing sugar, cream cheese, and vanilla extract into a bowl and whisk using a hand or electric whisk until smooth and thoroughly blended.

5 Spread half the icing on one cake, sit the other cake on top, and spread the remaining icing on top to make a swirl pattern. Decorate the top of the cake with the halved walnuts.

How I make the mixture

1 Put the oil, eggs, and sugar into a large mixing bowl. Whisk until the mixture is well combined, lighter, and noticeably thickened.

2 Gently fold the carrot into the cake batter, then stir in the flour, baking powder, mixed spice, ginger, and chopped walnuts until evenly blended.

Easy Fruit Cake

If you like a lighter fruit cake that still has lots of fruity flavour, this is a good "cut-and-come-again" one. Ideally, leave the cake a few days before eating, because then it will slice really well, whereas when it's very fresh it can crumble easily.

Ingredients

Serves 12

225g (8oz) butter (room temperature) or vegetable spread (at least 70% fat), plus extra for greasing
225g (8oz) caster sugar
4 large eggs
225g (8oz) self-raising flour
100g (3½oz) ground almonds
½ tsp almond extract
450g (1lb) mixed dried fruit
25g (scant 1oz) flaked almonds (optional)

PER SERVING

Calories: 458
Saturated fat: 6g
Unsaturated fat: 16g
Sodium: 268mg

STORING FRUIT CAKE

To store fruit cake, wrap it in greaseproof paper and then again in foil. If wrapped in this way, it will keep in an airtight tin for up to 2 weeks. Never put foil directly in contact with a fruit cake, as the acid in the fruit can cause the foil to corrode, impairing the flavour of the cake.

Method

1 Preheat the oven to 160°C (fan 140°C/325°F/Gas 3). Grease a 20cm (8in) springform or deep, loose-bottomed round cake tin. Line the base and sides of the tin with baking parchment.

2 In a large bowl, cream the butter or vegetable spread and sugar with an electric mixer or wooden spoon until fluffy, then add the eggs a little at a time, beating well between each addition to prevent curdling.

3 Fold in the flour, ground almonds, and almond extract and beat until all the ingredients are thoroughly mixed. Gently fold the dried fruit into the mixture, stirring with a wooden spoon until well combined.

4 Spoon the mixture into the tin and level the top. If you like, sprinkle the surface with the flaked almonds.

5 Put the tin into the oven and bake for 1½–2 hours. Test the cake for doneness as shown below. If the skewer comes out wet and sticky, return the cake to the oven to cook further. When the cake is done, remove from the oven and leave to cool in the tin.

Test the cake for doneness

To test if a fruit cake is cooked, insert a skewer in the centre of the cake: when withdrawn, it should be clean and dry, not wet or sticky.

"I've probably made over a thousand Victoria sponges, but I never tire of baking. It's relaxing, fun, and so rewarding to create something to share with family and friends."

Chocolate Brownies

Easy to mix, this all-in-one recipe makes brownies with a soft, cakey texture. It's a great family favourite that children love, and is perfect for when you want to make up a batch or more for birthday parties or bake sales.

Ingredients

Makes 12 squares

225g (8oz) butter (room temperature) or vegetable spread (at least 70% fat), plus extra for greasing
350g (12oz) light muscovado sugar
4 large eggs
50g (1¾oz) cocoa powder, sifted
250g (9oz) self-raising flour
85g (3oz) walnut pieces (optional)

FOR THE FROSTING

25g (scant 1oz) unsalted butter (room temperature), cubed
3 tbsp cocoa powder, sifted
225g (8oz) icing sugar, sifted

PER SERVING

Calories: 469
Saturated fat: 8g
Unsaturated fat: 13g
Sodium: 369mg

Method

1 Preheat the oven to 180°C (fan 160°C/350°F/Gas 4). Grease a traybake tin measuring 30 x 23cm (12 x 9in) and 4cm (1½in) deep and line the base of the tin with baking parchment.

2 Place the butter or vegetable spread, sugar, eggs, cocoa powder, and flour in a large bowl. Beat with an electric mixer on a low speed for about 3 minutes, or with a wooden spoon for a little longer, until smooth. Stir in the walnut pieces, if using.

3 Spoon the mixture into the tin, spread evenly, then bake for 40–45 minutes, covering with foil for the last 10 minutes.

4 Test for doneness by inserting a skewer into a brownie. If the skewer comes out clean, the brownies are ready. Leave to cool slightly in the tin, then turn out onto a wire rack to cool completely.

5 Make the frosting as shown below. Leave the frosting to cool before icing the brownies.

6 Spread the frosting evenly over the brownie base with a palette knife. Leave to set, then cut into 12 squares.

Make the chocolate frosting

In a bowl, soften the butter and add the cocoa powder. Gradually stir in 4 tablespoons of boiling water until smooth, then stir in the icing sugar.

Blueberry Muffins

Packed with blueberries, these traditional American muffins are nutritious as well as delicious. They are not over sweet – the lemon gives them a pleasingly tangy flavour – and are ideal for serving at breakfast or as a treat any time.

Ingredients

Makes 12

2 large eggs
85g (3oz) caster sugar
225ml (7½fl oz) milk
100g (3½oz) butter, melted and
    cooled a little
1 tsp vanilla extract
grated zest of 1 lemon
280g (9½oz) self-raising flour
1 tsp baking powder
225g (8oz) blueberries

PER SERVING

Calories: 200
Saturated fat: 5g
Unsaturated fat: 2g
Sodium: 211mg

Method

1 Preheat the oven to 200°C (fan 180°C/400°F/Gas 6). Line each hollow of a 12-hole muffin tin with a paper case.

2 Place the eggs in a large bowl. Add the sugar, milk, melted butter, vanilla extract, and lemon zest and stir to combine. Sift the flour and baking powder into the bowl.

3 Fold the ingredients together very roughly: this should not take more than 20 strokes, and the mixture should still look lumpy and uneven. Add the blueberries and stir them in, taking care not to bruise any fruits.

4 Divide the mixture equally between the 12 paper cases. Bake for 25–30 minutes, or until the muffins are well risen and splitting a little across the top.

5 Remove the muffins from the oven and place them on a wire rack. Leave them to cool a little, but they are best served warm.

Bake the muffins

1 Place the paper cases in the holes in the muffin tin. Spoon in the mixture, filling each case only to three-quarters full. Bake for 25–30 minutes.

2 Transfer the muffins to a wire rack to cool slightly. Ideally, serve while still warm, although they will keep in an airtight container for up to 2 days.

Fruity Scones

My favourite way to serve scones is split open, rather than sandwiched together. That way, you get lots of jam and cream. They're best served warm, or make them ahead and reheat in a low oven. For plain scones, simply omit the sultanas.

Ingredients

Makes 10

75g (2½ oz) butter, chilled and cut into cubes, plus extra for greasing
350g (12oz) self-raising flour, plus extra for dusting
1½ tsp baking powder
30g (1oz) caster sugar
75g (2½oz) sultanas
about 150ml (5fl oz) milk
2 large eggs, beaten

PER SERVING

Calories: 238
Saturated fat: 5g
Unsaturated fat: 4g
Sodium: 275mg

TIPS FOR GREAT SCONES

Scones need a light touch or they can become tough and heavy, so handle them as little as possible. Roll them out quite thickly to start with; they never rise as much as you think they will. As the dough is quite deep, dip the cutter in flour before cutting out each scone to prevent the dough from sticking to it.

Method

1 Preheat the oven to 220°C (fan 200°C/425°F/Gas 7). Lightly grease a large baking sheet.

2 Mix the flour, baking powder, and butter cubes, as shown below, then stir in the sugar and sultanas.

3 Pour 100ml (3½fl oz) of the milk and all but 2 tablespoons of the beaten egg into the flour mixture. Mix together with a round-bladed knife to a soft, but not too sticky dough, adding a bit more milk if needed to mop up any dry bits of mixture in the bottom of the bowl.

4 Turn the dough out onto a lightly floured work surface, lightly knead just a few times only until gathered together, then gently roll and pat out to form a rectangle about 2cm (¾in) deep.

5 Cut out as many rounds as possible from the first rolling with a 6cm (2½in) cutter (a plain cutter is easier to use than a fluted one) and lay them on the baking sheet, spaced slightly apart. Gather the trimmings, then roll and cut out again. Repeat until you have 10 scones.

6 Brush the tops of the scones with the reserved egg. Bake for about 10 minutes, or until risen and golden. Remove and cool on a wire rack.

Make a light, crumbly dough

1 Put the flour and baking powder into a large chilled mixing bowl. Add the cubes of butter, keeping all the ingredients as cold as possible.

2 Rub in lightly and quickly with your fingertips until the mixture looks like fine breadcrumbs. Add the sugar, sultanas, milk, and egg.

Sultana Flapjacks

Children love to find one of these flapjacks tucked in their lunch box. Just cut them a small square and include some fresh fruit. Bake a big batch of them; if stored in an airtight tin they'll last for up to a week – if they're not eaten first!

Ingredients

Makes 24 squares

225g (8oz) butter, plus
   extra for greasing
225g (8oz) demerara sugar
75g (2½oz) golden syrup
350g (12oz) porridge oats
100g (3½oz) sultanas

PER SERVING

Calories: 170
Saturated fat: 5g
Unsaturated fat: 4g
Sodium: 73mg

Method

1 Preheat the oven to 160°C (fan 140°C/325°F/Gas 3). Grease a traybake tin measuring 30 x 23cm (12 x 9in) and 4cm (1½in) deep, and line the base with baking parchment.

2 Put the butter, sugar, and golden syrup into a large pan and place over a medium-low heat. When melted, remove from the heat and stir in the oats and sultanas.

3 Spoon the oat mixture from the pan into the prepared tin. Press down firmly with the back of a spoon and level the surface.

4 Bake for about 35 minutes until pale golden brown; you may need to turn the tin halfway through cooking to ensure even cooking.

5 Leave to cool for about 10 minutes, then cut the flapjacks into 24 squares using a sharp knife.

6 Leave in the tin to cool completely, then lever the flapjacks out of the tin using a fish slice.

VARIATION Cranberry Flapjacks You can replace the sultanas with the same quantity of dried cranberries.

Prepare the tin

Lightly butter the base and sides of the tin. Line the base of the tin with baking parchment.

Make foolproof flapjacks

1 In a large pan on the hob, melt the butter, sugar, and syrup, stirring constantly with a wooden spoon.

2 Remove from the heat and add the oats. Stir until well coated, then add the sultanas. Do not over-work the mix.

Mary's Secrets of Success

Cakes and Biscuits

1 Be sure to use the specified size of cake tin. Even the difference of 1cm (½in) all round can mean the difference between success and failure.

2 If using a fat other than butter, make sure it is suitable for baking. It must be made of at least 70 per cent fat; low-fat spreads are not suitable because of their high water content.

Chocolate Brownies, pp308–309

3 If you find your cakes don't rise it could be caused by a number of factors, including insufficient raising agent, too cool an oven, or too stiff a mixture. Always follow the instructions in the recipe carefully.

4 Measure baking powder precisely, as too much can create a bitter or dry result, or cause the cake to rise up and fall back down, making an unsightly dip in the surface.

5 Place cake tins on the middle rack of the oven at the right temperature. Cakes baked on the top shelf will crack.

Blueberry Muffins, pp310–11

6 When arranging biscuits on a baking sheet, leave enough space between them to allow for spreading. If I'm making more biscuits than fit on my baking sheets, I just cook them in batches – they don't take long.

Chocolate-chip Cookies, pp318-19

7 Bake for the minimum time given in the recipe before opening the oven door. If the door is opened too soon it may cause some cakes to deflate.

8 If a cake looks as though it's browning too quickly, I cover the top loosely with foil. Cakes that are baked for too long will be dry and the outside will be crisp.

9 Most biscuits can be stored in an airtight tin for a few days. If they soften, crisp them up in a warm oven.

10 Do not store cakes and biscuits together, as the moisture from the cakes will soften the biscuits.

Victoria Sandwich Cake, pp292-95

Chocolate-chip Cookies

These are family-size cookies, but you could make them slightly smaller and bake for a little less time if you want to serve them alongside a pudding, such as vanilla or chocolate ice cream. To keep the cookies fresh, store them in an airtight tin.

Ingredients

Makes 24

85g (3oz) butter (room temperature) or vegetable spread (at least 70% fat), plus extra for greasing
100g (3½oz) caster sugar
1 large egg, beaten
175g (6oz) self-raising flour
½ tsp vanilla extract
50g (1¾oz) plain dark chocolate chips
50g (1¾oz) chopped nuts, such as blanched almonds

PER SERVING

Calories: 94
Saturated fat: 2g
Unsaturated fat: 3g
Sodium: 65mg

Method

1 Preheat the oven to 180°C (fan 160°C/350°F/Gas 4). Lightly grease a baking sheet. If necessary, use one sheet and bake in batches.

2 Place the butter or vegetable spread, sugar, egg, flour, and vanilla extract in a large bowl. Beat with an electric mixer for 2 minutes, or with a wooden spoon for a little longer, until the dough is a smooth consistency. Stir in the chocolate chips and nuts.

3 Divide the dough into thirds (each third should yield 8 cookies). Place large teaspoonfuls of the dough onto the baking sheet as shown below; you will probably get 8 cookies on the sheet at a time. With the back of the spoon, flatten each mound into a round about 5cm (2in) across.

4 Bake for 15–20 minutes, or until pale golden brown with slightly darker edges. The cookies will be just firm to the touch. Lift carefully off the baking sheet with a palette knife and transfer to a wire rack to cool.

5 Wipe the baking sheet, let it cool, and grease it again before baking the next batch of cookies in the same way.

Spoon out the dough

Place spoonfuls of the dough onto a baking sheet, spacing the mounds 7–8cm (3in) apart. Use your finger or another spoon to scrape the mixture off the spoon. Flatten the mounds.

Shortbread

To give shortbread its true flavour, it must be made with butter. For the slightly crunchy texture, it needs to be cooked right through, so before you take it out of the oven, check that the underneath is a light biscuit colour as well as the top.

Ingredients

Makes 12 slices

75g (2½oz) ground rice or semolina

175g (6oz) plain flour, plus extra
   for dusting

175g (6oz) butter (room temperature),
   cut into cubes

75g (2½oz) caster sugar, plus extra
   for sprinkling

PER SERVING

Calories: 205
Saturated fat: 8g
Unsaturated fat: 4g
Sodium: 90mg

SHORTBREAD TIPS

Ground rice or semolina gives shortbread a subtle, gritty consistency, but for a smoother texture you can use cornflour instead. The dough binds together more easily if the butter is soft rather than using it straight from the fridge. There's no need to grease the baking sheet, as there's enough butter in the dough for it not to stick while baking.

Method

1 Put the ground rice or semolina into a large bowl with the flour. Add the butter and rub it in as shown below.

2 Stir in the sugar, then press and knead the mixture together until it forms a smooth, round ball.

3 On a lightly floured work surface, roll the dough out to a 25cm (10in) round. Slide it onto a large, round baking sheet.

4 Crimp the edges with your fingers, or press them with the back of a fork to decorate. Prick the surface all over with a fork, then mark into 12 triangles with a sharp knife. Chill until firm, about 30 minutes. Meanwhile, preheat the oven to 160°C (fan 140°C/325°F/Gas 3).

5 Bake for 30–35 minutes, or until pale golden brown. Remove from the oven and, while still warm, cut through the wedge markings and sprinkle with a little extra sugar.

6 Leave the shortbread to cool on the baking sheet for approximately 5 minutes, then lift off carefully with a palette knife and transfer to a wire rack to cool completely. Store in an airtight container.

Make a crumbly, butter-rich dough

1 Tip the cubes of soft butter into the bowl containing the flour and ground rice or semolina.

2 With your fingertips, rub in the butter. When the mix resembles coarse bread-crumbs, add the sugar and combine.

Chocolate Éclairs

Not many can resist an éclair, and these are just the right size. If you want to flavour and sweeten the cream, stir in a little vanilla extract and caster sugar. Serve the éclairs as soon as possible after filling, or the pastry will go soggy.

Ingredients

Makes 12

50g (1¾oz) butter, cut into cubes, plus extra for greasing
75g (2½oz) plain flour
2 large eggs, beaten
300ml (10fl oz) double or whipping cream

FOR THE ICING

100g (3½oz) plain dark chocolate (about 40% cocoa solids), finely chopped
100ml (3½fl oz) double cream

PER SERVING

Calories: 277
Saturated fat: 15g
Unsaturated fat: 10g
Sodium: 50mg

Method

1 Preheat the oven to 220°C (fan 200°C/425°F/Gas 7). Grease a large baking sheet. Make the éclair mixture (choux pastry) as shown below.

2 Spoon the mixture into a large piping bag fitted with a 1cm (½in) plain nozzle. Sprinkle the baking sheet with water (a water spray with a fine nozzle is good for this). Pipe the mixture onto the baking sheet into 7.5cm (3in) lengths, leaving room between each éclair for them to spread a bit.

3 Bake for 10 minutes, then reduce the heat to 190°C (fan 170°C/375°F/ Gas 5) and bake for a further 20 minutes. Split each éclair in half lengthways and transfer to a wire rack to cool completely.

4 Make the icing: put the chocolate and double cream in a heatproof bowl and set it over a pan of gently simmering water, stirring until smooth and shiny. Remove the bowl from the pan and leave the icing at room temperature for about 30–35 minutes, or until it is cool and thick enough to coat the éclairs without dripping off them.

5 Once the éclairs have cooled, whip the cream and spoon or pipe it into the bottom half of the éclairs. Dip the top half of each éclair in the icing, then place on top of the whipped cream.

Make lovely light choux pastry

1 Put the butter in a heavy-based pan with 150ml (5fl oz) water and heat until the butter melts. Bring to the boil, tip in the flour, then remove from the heat. Stir vigorously.

2 When a smooth paste develops, return the pan to the heat, stirring. The mixture will dry out a little and form a soft ball that comes away from the sides of the pan.

3 Remove the pan from the heat again, leave the mixture to cool slightly, then gradually add the eggs, beating really well between each addition until the mixture is smooth and glossy.

Bread

Master Recipe

Three-seed Crown Loaf

Even if you've never made bread before, this simple recipe will enable you to make a loaf to be proud of the first time you try. It uses fast-action dried yeast, which is easier and quicker to use than fresh yeast. Always aim for a wet dough, as it gives better results.

Makes 8 bread rolls   **Prep** 25 mins, plus 2–2½ hours rising   **Cook** 30 mins

Ingredients

500g (1lb 2oz) strong wholemeal flour, plus extra for dusting
2 tsp salt
7g sachet easy-blend (fast-action) dried yeast
2 tbsp clear honey
2 tbsp sunflower oil, plus extra for greasing
125g (4½oz) sunflower seeds
25g (scant 1oz) poppy seeds
25g (scant 1oz) sesame seeds

Special equipment
23cm (9in) springform or loose-bottomed round cake tin

PER SERVING
Calories: 265
Saturated fat: 1g
Unsaturated fat: 7g
Sodium: 393mg

Cook's notes

Alternative toppings
You can vary the loaf's toppings according to what you have in your storecupboard. Try porridge oats or caraway seeds, for instance.

Prepare ahead
You can make the dough a day ahead. After covering the bowl with cling film, place it in the fridge and leave overnight. Remove and let it stand until it doubles in size, then continue from "Finish the loaf".

Make the dough

Prep 5 mins

KEY to SUCCESS Always use strong flour, as it makes the dough more elastic.

1 Measure the flour, salt, and yeast into a large bowl. Pour over 300ml (10fl oz) hand-warm water, then add the honey and oil.

2 Mix to form a soft, sticky dough. It should be wet enough to cling to the bowl: add more tepid water if needed. Turn out onto a lightly floured surface.

Knead the dough

Prep 10 mins, plus
about 1½ hours rising

KEY to SUCCESS Knead the dough thoroughly, either by hand or using a dough hook.

1 Knead the dough for 10 minutes: use the weight of your body to push down with the heel of your hand into the dough and then stretch it out away from your body.

2 Fold the end of the dough back to the top. Give the dough a quarter turn and repeat, building up a smooth rocking action. Rub oil round the inside of a large bowl.

KEY to SUCCESS Bread will rise best at a temperature of about 25°C (77°F); an airing cupboard is ideal.

3 Put the dough into the oiled bowl, then cover the bowl with cling film. Leave in a warm place for about 1½ hours, or until the dough has doubled in size. Bread will rise at any temperature, but it will be considerably faster in a warm environment.

Finish the loaf

Prep 10 mins, plus 40 mins rising

Cook About 30 mins

1 Turn out the dough and pat flat. Scatter with 100g (3½oz) of the sunflower seeds, then roll up and knead for 20–30 turns. Make a round, cut into 8 wedges, then roll into balls.

2 Dip 3 balls in poppy seeds, 2 in sesame, 2 in sunflower, 1 in flour. Grease the tin, insert the balls, and let rise for 40 minutes. Preheat oven to 230°C (fan 210°C/450°F/Gas 8).

KEY to SUCCESS Be sure to test that the loaf is fully cooked before cooling.

3 Bake for 10 minutes. Lower the heat to 200°C (fan 180°C/400°F/Gas 6), and bake for a further 20 minutes. Test to see if the loaf is cooked: remove it from its tin and tap the base; it should sound hollow. If not, place it upside down in the oven for a few minutes. Cool on a wire rack.

"I love the different textures and tastes of the seeds in this loaf, and they look so pretty too."

Farmhouse Loaf

Once you've mastered this classic white loaf you can try out the variations, such as olive or sun-dried tomato bread. When mixing the dough, it's better to have it on the moist side. If the mixture sticks to your hands, you'll probably make a good loaf.

Ingredients

Makes 1 loaf

500g (1lb 2oz) strong white flour, plus extra for dusting

7g sachet easy-blend (fast-action) dried yeast

2 tsp salt

1 tbsp sunflower oil, plus extra for greasing

PER LOAF

Calories: 1895
Saturated fat: 3g
Unsaturated fat: 22g
Sodium: 3126mg

WATER QUANTITIES

I can only ever give a guide to the amount of liquid to be used in bread-making, because the absorbency of flour can vary considerably. The quantity of liquid that flour can absorb depends on temperature, humidity, and the brand of flour you use. Aim for a slightly sticky dough; it must not be dry.

Method

1 Put the flour, yeast, and salt into a large bowl. Pour in 300ml (10fl oz) hand-warm water and the oil. Using a round-bladed knife, mix to a soft dough. Add 2–3 teaspoons more hand-warm water if necessary. Gather the dough into a ball.

2 Turn the dough out onto a lightly floured surface and knead for 8–10 minutes until it feels smooth and elastic.

3 Turn the dough into a large, lightly oiled bowl. Cover the bowl with cling film. Leave to rise in a warm place for about 1½ hours, or until the dough doubles in size.

4 Lightly grease and line the base of a 900g (2lb) loaf tin measuring 20 x 10.5cm (8 x 4½in) and 6cm (2½in) deep with baking parchment. Turn the risen dough onto a lightly floured surface and knead 3 or 4 times. Pat or roll it into a 20 x 18cm (8 x 7in) rectangle.

5 Roll up the dough from one long side. With the seam underneath, drop it into the tin. Cover loosely with oiled cling film and leave to rise in a warm place for about 30 minutes, or until risen just above the edges of tin.

6 Preheat the oven to 230°C (fan 210°C/450°F/Gas 8). Dust the loaf with flour and bake for 10 minutes, then reduce the oven temperature to 200°C (fan 180°C/400°F/Gas 6) and bake for a further 30–40 minutes or until golden brown.

7 Turn the loaf out of the tin and tap it on the bottom: it should sound hollow. If not, place it upside down in the oven for a few more minutes. Cool the loaf on a wire rack.

VARIATIONS **Olive Bread** Make the dough as in steps 1–3 of the main recipe, but replace the sunflower oil with olive oil. In step 4, work in 100g (3½oz) black and green olives, stoned and chopped, kneading them firmly into the dough until they are evenly distributed. Continue as in the main recipe.

Sun-dried Tomato Bread Drain 100g (3½oz) sun-dried tomatoes in olive oil, reserving the oil. Chop the tomatoes roughly. Make the dough as in steps 1–3 of the main recipe, using the oil from the tomatoes instead of sunflower oil. In step 4, work in the chopped tomatoes, kneading them firmly into the dough until they are evenly distributed. Continue as in the main recipe.

Cheese and Caramelized Onion Loaves

These impressive-looking loaves are full of flavour, both inside and on top. They are delicious served warm or cold, are ideal for taking on a picnic, and make the perfect accompaniment for soup or a selection of cheeses.

Ingredients

Makes 2 small loaves

500g (1lb 2oz) strong white flour, plus extra for dusting

7g sachet easy-blend (fast-action) dried yeast

1½ tsp salt

25g (scant 1oz) butter (room temperature)

100g (3½oz) mature Cheddar cheese, grated

25g (scant 1oz) Parmesan cheese, grated

sunflower oil, for greasing

FOR THE TOPPING

1 tbsp olive oil

2 small onions, peeled and very thinly sliced

salt and freshly ground black pepper

30g (1oz) mature Cheddar cheese, grated

beaten egg, to glaze

PER LOAF

Calories: 1397
Saturated fat: 25g
Unsaturated fat: 24g
Sodium: 1872mg

Method

1 Put the flour, yeast, and salt into a large bowl with the butter. Rub the butter into the flour then stir in both cheeses. Make a well in the middle and, using a round-bladed knife, stir in 300ml (10fl oz) hand-warm water, then up to 60ml (2fl oz) more as needed to mix to a soft, slightly sticky dough. Gather the dough into a ball.

2 Knead the dough on a lightly floured surface for 8–10 minutes until it feels smooth and elastic. Shape the dough into a round. Turn the dough into a large, lightly oiled bowl, then cover with cling film. Leave in a warm place for about 1¼–2 hours, or until doubled in size.

3 Meanwhile, make the topping: heat the oil in a large frying pan, tip in the onions, and fry over a medium heat for 10–12 minutes, stirring occasionally, until softened and lightly caramelized, but not very brown. Lower the heat if they start to brown too quickly. Remove, season with salt and pepper, and leave to cool.

4 Line a large baking sheet with baking parchment. Turn the dough onto a lightly floured surface and knead 3 or 4 times. Too much handling now will lose the dough's lightness.

5 Cut the dough in half and shape each half into a ball. Place well apart on the lined baking sheet. Slash the tops of each one about 5 times with a sharp knife.

6 Cover loosely with oiled cling film and leave to rise in a warm place for about 40 minutes–1 hour, or until doubled in size. Preheat the oven to 220°C (fan 200°C/425°F/Gas 7).

7 Brush each loaf with the beaten egg, scatter the onion over, then the 30g (1oz) of grated cheese. Bake the loaves for 10 minutes, then reduce the oven temperature to 200°C (fan 180°C/400°F/Gas 6) and bake for a further 20–25 minutes until golden brown. Cover loosely with foil for the last 5 minutes if the onions are getting too brown.

8 Tap the base of each loaf to see if they are cooked: they should sound hollow. Place on a wire rack to cool.

Rosemary and Garlic Focaccia

As this traditional Italian bread has so much flavour from the sea salt, rosemary, and garlic topping, it is lovely just as it is – there's no need for butter. Try serving it as a starter for sharing, with oil and balsamic vinegar for dipping. Best served warm.

Ingredients

Makes 1 loaf

450g (1lb) strong white flour,
   plus extra for dusting
7g sachet easy-blend (fast-action)
   dried yeast
1 tsp salt
2 tbsp olive oil, plus extra for greasing

FOR THE TOPPING

1 tbsp olive oil
1 rounded tsp sea salt flakes
2 garlic cloves, peeled and thinly sliced
1-2 stalks of fresh rosemary,
   leaves removed
extra virgin olive oil, for drizzling

PER LOAF

Calories: 2029
Saturated fat: 9g
Unsaturated fat: 52g
Sodium: 3158mg

TIPS FOR GREAT FOCACCIA

Focaccia dough should be very soft and requires light handling to retain the characteristic air bubbles: when kneading, move the ball of dough around in your cupped hands on the work surface, tucking the edges under as you go. When transferring the rolled-out dough to the baking sheet, you may find it easier to drape the dough over the rolling pin first.

Method

1 Mix the flour in a large bowl with the yeast and the salt. Make a well in the middle, add the oil then gradually pour in 300ml (10fl oz) hand-warm water, adding up to 60ml (2fl oz) more as needed.

2 Transfer the dough to a lightly floured work surface and knead gently for 8–10 minutes until smooth. Small air bubbles will appear on the surface. Put the dough in a large, lightly oiled bowl, cover, and leave in a warm place for 50 minutes–1 hour, or until doubled in size.

3 When risen, gently knead the dough on the work surface 4 or 5 times, being careful not to knock out the air. Cover and leave for 10 minutes.

4 Lightly grease a large baking sheet. Roll out (or roll and gently pull) the dough to a rectangle about 30 x 23cm (12 x 9in) and 1cm (½in) thick, again being careful not to knock out the air bubbles. Lift the dough onto the baking sheet, ease it back into shape if necessary, then cover with a clean tea towel and leave for 25–35 minutes, or until doubled in size. Preheat the oven to 200°C (fan 180°C/400°F/Gas 6).

5 Make dimples over the top of the dough with your fingers. Brush with most of the olive oil, then scatter over the sea salt, garlic, and rosemary leaves. Brush these with the rest of the oil. Bake for 25 minutes until golden. Drizzle with a little oil and transfer to a wire rack to cool slightly.

Cover the dough

After the first rising, knead the dough again a few times, then cover with a clean tea towel. Leave for 10 minutes.

Mary's Secrets of Success

Bread

1 **The best flour for making yeast dough** is labelled "strong flour". You can use ordinary plain flour, but the result will be a more close-textured, crumbly loaf.

Three-seed Crown Loaf, pp326-29

2 **If you're new to bread-making,** I recommend you use easy-blend dried yeast (also known as fast-action), as it is simpler and quicker to deal with than fresh or ordinary dried yeast.

3 **It's always tricky to gauge the quantity** of liquid required for bread dough, because the absorbency of flour can vary. For a good result, the dough should be sticky. If it's too dry your bread will be dry, so add a little more liquid if necessary.

Rosemary and Garlic Focaccia, pp334-35

4 **Dough rises quickest in a warm environment,** for instance an airing cupboard or a warm kitchen. However, it will rise at most temperatures; some people leave it in the fridge overnight.

5 **To test if dough has risen,** push in a finger; when you withdraw it, an indentation should remain in the dough.

6 You can use an electric mixer fitted with a dough hook or food processor for making bread dough.

7 Make sure you use a really hot oven for bread-baking; don't put the bread in until the oven has reached the desired temperature. For a crisp crust, put a bowl of water in an ovenproof bowl to create steam.

Farmhouse Loaf, pp330–31

8 To test if a loaf is cooked, I tip it out of the tin and tap its base. The bread should have a hollow-drum-like sound.

9 Bread freezes well. Pack loaves in moisture-proof wrapping and seal tightly. Most loaves can be frozen for up to 4 months; if enriched with milk or fruit, storage time is 3 months. Thaw, still wrapped, at room temperature.

Cheese and Caramelized Onion Loaves, pp332–33

10 I sometimes add a glaze to my loaves. Apply the glaze thinly before baking using a pastry brush. For a crisp crust, brush with water; for a soft crust, use milk or cream; for a shiny crust, apply egg yolk beaten with a pinch of salt.

Walnut and Raisin Loaf

An ideal breakfast bread, this is also delicious toasted. Just spread it with butter or eat it on its own; it doesn't need anything else. If you're allergic to nuts, replace them with snipped, dried apricots. For freezing, cut it into slices first.

Ingredients

Makes 1 loaf

500g (1lb 2oz) strong white flour, plus extra for dusting

7g sachet easy-blend (fast-action) dried yeast

2 tsp caster sugar

1 tsp salt

1 tsp ground cinnamon

25g (scant 1oz) butter (room temperature)

sunflower oil, for greasing

60g (2oz) walnuts, chopped

60g (2oz) raisins

FOR THE GLAZE

1 tbsp caster sugar

large pinch of ground cinnamon

PER LOAF

Calories: 2484
Saturated fat: 18g
Unsaturated fat: 50g
Sodium: 190mg

Method

1 Put the flour, yeast, sugar, salt, and cinnamon into a large bowl with the butter. Rub the butter into the flour. Make a well in the middle and, using a round-bladed knife, stir in about 300ml (10fl oz) hand-warm water to mix to a soft, slightly sticky dough. Gather the dough into a ball.

2 Knead the dough on a lightly floured surface for 8–10 minutes, or until it feels smooth and elastic. Shape the dough into a round.

3 Turn the dough into a large, lightly oiled bowl. Cover with cling film and leave to rise in a warm place for 1–1½ hours, or until doubled in size.

4 Lightly grease and line the base of a 900g (2lb) loaf tin measuring 20 x 10.5cm (8 x 4½in) and 6cm (2½in) deep with baking parchment. Turn the risen dough out onto a lightly floured surface and knead just 3 or 4 times. Too much handling now will lose the dough's lightness.

5 Flatten and gently stretch the dough into a rectangle about 28 x 18cm (11 x 7in). Scatter the walnuts and raisins evenly over, press them lightly in, then roll up tightly from the short ends.

6 Place the dough in the oiled tin with the seam underneath. Cover loosely with oiled cling film and leave to rise in a warm place for 40–50 minutes, or until the dough reaches just above the top of the tin. Preheat the oven to 220°C (fan 200°C/425°F/Gas 7).

7 Meanwhile, make the glaze: mix the sugar and cinnamon with 1 teaspoon of hot water. Set aside.

8 Bake the loaf for 10 minutes, then reduce the oven temperature to 200°C (fan 180°C/400°F/Gas 6) and bake for a further 20–25 minutes until the surface is golden brown.

9 Turn the loaf out of the tin and tap the base to see if it is cooked: it should sound hollow. If not, place it upside down in the oven for a few more minutes. Place on a wire rack and brush with the glaze while the loaf is still warm. Leave to cool.

Pepperoni Pizza

Pizza is a really good stand-by for children's tea. With all the topping possibilities, it's such a versatile recipe. Try scattering roasted vegetables over the top (see pp204–207) instead of pepperoni. Tuna and anchovies also make good toppings.

Ingredients

Makes 2

250g (9oz) strong white flour, plus extra for dusting

½ x 7g sachet easy-blend (fast-action) dried yeast

1 tsp salt

1 tbsp olive oil, plus extra for greasing

FOR THE TOPPING

150g packet mozzarella cheese

6 tbsp sun-dried tomato paste

50g (1¾oz) pepperoni, thinly sliced

25g (scant 1oz) grated Parmesan cheese

2 tbsp sliced pickled mild chillies

2 tbsp olive oil

½ tsp dried marjoram or 1 tbsp fresh, finely chopped parsley

PER SERVING

Calories: 982
Saturated fat: 19g
Unsaturated fat: 29.5g
Sodium: 1740mg

Method

1 Measure the flour, yeast, and salt into a large bowl. Pour in 150ml (5fl oz) hand-warm water and 1 tablespoon oil and mix to a soft dough. Add 2–3 teaspoons more water, if necessary.

2 Turn the dough out onto a lightly floured surface and knead for about 10 minutes as shown in step 1, below. Place the dough in a large, lightly oiled bowl. Cover the bowl with cling film and leave in a warm place for about 1½ hours, or until the dough doubles in size.

3 Grease two baking sheets. Knead the dough for a few minutes, then divide in half. Make two pizza bases as shown in step 2, below.

4 Drain the mozzarella and slice thinly. Spread the tomato paste over each pizza, avoiding the border, then top with the mozzarella. Arrange the pepperoni over the mozzarella and sprinkle the cheese and chillies on top. Sprinkle with the oil and marjoram or parsley. Set aside to rest.

5 Preheat the oven to 230°C (fan 210°C/450°F/Gas 8). Bake for about 10 minutes, or until the pizza edges are crisp and golden, swapping the sheets over halfway so they get even cooking.

Make the pizza base

1 To knead the dough, fold it over towards you, then push it down and away with the heel of your hand. Turn the dough and repeat. Continue for 10 minutes until smooth and elastic.

2 Roll and stretch the dough until it is about 23–25cm (9–10in) round and about 1cm (½in) thick. Make a rim around the edge. Place on a greased baking sheet and add the topping.

Index

Index

Index

Index

Index

Index

Acknowledgments

About the author

Mary Berry is one of the UK's most loved and respected cookery writers and bakers. She is also widely known as a judge on the hit BBC2 TV programme *The Great British Bake-off* and is the author of over 80 cookbooks, with 6 million sales worldwide, including the bestselling *Mary Berry's Complete Cookbook* (DK), which has sold over a million copies. Mary Berry knows the joy of becoming a confident cook and distils a lifetime of her cooking experience in this course.

Mary Berry would like to thank

Firstly, Lucy Young is not only my best friend of too many years to count, but the best assistant working with me. She is full of ideas, and having young friends she knows exactly what the modern cook wants. Together we seek perfection for all the recipes. Angela Nilsen has meticulously tested the new recipes, making them clear and easy to follow, and resulting in foolproof recipes. Thank you, Angela – you have been a joy to work with. Huge thank you to Polly Boyd for editing this book; never a moan when we would change something at the last minute, total dedication to making this book perfect – we are constantly giving her gold stars! Thanks also to Dawn Henderson and Katherine Raj at DK, to home economists Jane Lawrie and Penny Stephens, and to Tony Briscoe for the lovely photographs.

DK would like to thank

Angela Nilsen for assisting Mary Berry with recipe development and testing, Lucy Young for recipe consultation, Fiona Hunter for nutritional analyses, Susan Downing, Geoff Fennell, and Lisa Pettibone for Art Direction, Liz Hippisley and Wei Tang for prop styling, Steve Crozier for retouching, Boo Attwood for wardrobe styling, Jo Penford for hair and make-up, Elizabeth Yeates and Elizabeth Clinton for editorial assistance, Corinne Masciocchi for proofreading, and Vanessa Bird for indexing.